THE MOTOR BUS SERVICES OF KENT AND EAST SUSSEX
– A Brief History

by Eric Baldock

Published by Meresborough Books

INTRODUCTION

This book traces the history of bus and coach services within the area now served by East Kent, Maidstone & District, Hastings & District and the Kentish operations of London Country. The original concept was to deal purely with Kent, but the penetration of M & D and East Kent deep into East Sussex is an integral part of the story that must be included. Conversely London Transport and its forerunners are well covered elsewhere and consideration here is accordingly limited.

The first motor buses were on the whole unreliable and many services failed because the make of vehicle chosen did not live up to expectations; some operators were lucky enough to pick more reliable types (like the Milnes-Daimler), but even this did not prevent financial collapse or withdrawal due to poor roads. By about 1910 motor buses had improved enough to bring costs down and begin to oust horse-power. The Great War curtailed many operations, but the release of improved designs and ex-military chassis gave rise to the rapid expansion and fierce competition of the roaring twenties. Many firms were short-lived, selling-out to the large (territorial) companies as competition became too intense. Government concern at this chaos led to legislation to control the industry (1924 & 1933 in London and 1930 nationally), and this hastened the end of many operators in the early thirties. A period of stability was again shattered by war, affecting operations drastically, particularly in Kent.

The post-war boom in traffic gave the industry some of its best years, but demand was already falling when the Suez Crisis of 1956 caused a reduction of services, many of which were never restored; increasing numbers of cars and televisions being the main reason for this decline. Despite cuts in services and increased one-man-operation, profits dwindled; nationalisation finally came in 1968 and since then the industry has had to rely on council subsidies to break even and, alas, has been subject to political dogma.

Many routes have been reduced to a basic service for work, shopping or school, with no evening or Sunday facility, and recently some services have been taken-over by independent operators with lower overheads than the nationalised sector.

On the brighter side, the Transport Act 1980 has resulted in a number of new longer-distance routes, especially to London, and rekindled a spirit of competition on certain routes that had not been seen since the thirties.

A book of this size can only pick out the more significant and interesting aspects of this complex story but I trust the reader, whether transport enthusiast or historian, will find this account of value. The text is correct to late summer 1984.

Eric Baldock MCIT
Maidstone
December 1984

ACKNOWLEDGEMENTS AND SOURCES

This book would not have been possible without the work over the years of many enthusiasts who have recorded information, hoarded old timetables, taken photographs and published articles and books. To name all these people is impossible, and I trust all those not mentioned specifically will accept my thanks and forgive me for their omission.

By far the most important source of material has been the publications and records of the M & D and East Kent Bus Club. The Club was formed in 1952 and over the years its monthly news-sheet (edited by Don Vincent, then Paul Hollingsbee and currently Nicholas King) and many publications, including the M & D Fleet History (1977), the East Kent Fleet History (1978) and 75 Years of Municipal Transport in Maidstone (1979), have produced a vast quantity of data on these operators and their forerunners. Its extensive timetable library has also been invaluable when my own collection proved inadequate.

Similarly the publications of the London Omnibus Traction Society, especially the annual London Bus Review and London's Independent Bus Services (1978), have been of great use for the operations in the Kentish fringes of the capital.

The Tramways of Kent by 'Invicta' published in two volumes by the Light Railway League (1971/5) gives much detail of bus services of the erstwhile tram fleets.

The History of British Bus Services — Vol.1 — South East England by Colin Morris (Transport Publishing Co 1980) was a milestone when published, but even since then further information has come to light. This includes Dave Bubier's research into the early operators in the Herne Bay area (to which he has kindly allowed me access), and my own interview with Mr A. Standen, formerly of Sheppey Motor Transport.

Bob Cook's knowledge of early M & D services, especially in Sussex, and Nicholas King's detailed records have both been called upon to check various anomalies, some of which have still to be resolved!

The companies' own publications have also been consulted; these include the East Kent Omnibus staff magazine and their Jubilee Brochure (1966) and M & D's 50 Years of Service (1961) together with their staff magazine 'The Green 'Un' and later 'Inside Only'.

Other sources providing information on local bus services include the Golden Age of Buses by C.F. Klapper (Routledge & Kegan Paul 1978), the History of British Trolleybuses by Nicholas Owen (David & Charles 1974), A History of London Transport by T.C. Barker and Michael Robbins (George Allen & Unwin 1974), 50 Years of Greenline by K. Warren (Ian Allan 1980) and East Surrey by 'Bell Street' (HJ Publications 1974). One of the joint authors of the latter book, John King, has also produced a detailed history of early service in Tunbridge Wells, published by the Omnibus Society.

The monthly 'Buses' magazine (Ian Allan) has through its many issues featured items on Kent, including Orpington Independents by J.M. Austin (Dec 1976), Kent and Sussex by Bus by D. Trevor Rowe (Oct 1965), Eden Valley Village Bus by John Parke (May 1979) and Maidstone Area Coordination by myself (Nov 1981). Mark Rye's article in Buses Extra 22, The Bexhill Effect, gives a fuller story of the new independent operators in East Sussex, and Buses Extra 12 features Ian Paterson's Maidstone Borough Council — The First Five Years.

Many of the pictures in this book are from my camera or from my ever growing collection of contemporary postcards, and it includes vehicles never before illustrated, like Autocar's ABC and Wills' MMC. The source of other photographs is credited at the end of its caption, although it does not necessarily denote the holder of the copyright, which is often uncertain on the older views; a small royalty fee is available to those who can show copyright and have not already received or waived it.

Special thanks are due to Richard Lewis, Photographic Officer of the M & D and East Kent Bus Club, for his work in searching the club's vast collection for use in this book. This collection includes many early official views originally held by M & D and East Kent; readers wishing to obtain postcard photographs of these fleets should write to the Club at 42 St Alban's Hill, Hemel Hempstead, Herts, HP3 9NG. Prints from my collection are also available from this source.

I would finally like to thank the publicity department of London Transport for permission to use the pictures from their archives, and all the various company officials who have over the years aided the enthusiast movement.

The author would be pleased to hear from anyone who has any information on early bus services in the area, especially any old timetables, press cuttings, photos, or tickets.

Published by Meresborough Books, 7 Station Road, Rainham, GILLINGHAM, Kent ME8 7RS

© Copyright 1985 Eric Baldock

ISBN 0905270 959

Printed by Mackays of Chatham Ltd

BACK COVER: East Kent and M & D route maps from the early sixties: the networks were basically unchanged from 1933 until NBC days.

FRONT COVER: Standing by their M & D Tilling-Stevens at Seal during World War I are one of the earliest husband and wife bus crews in Kent. In contrast Driver and Conductress Bassom prepare to work the last East Kent journey scheduled for crew operation, the 1815 from Canterbury on the Whitstable/ Herne Bay circular on 25th July 1981, using AEC Regent GJG 733 D.

(top: M & D and East Kent Bus Club)

Horse buses on Ongley's Maidstone to Sittingbourne service cross at the Three Squirrels Inn, Stockbury.   (Irene Hales Collection)

THE HORSE BUS ERA

The bus evolved from three distinct predecessors; the stage-coach which carried pre-booked passengers to a fixed timetable, the hackney carriage which plied for hire within a given area, and the carrier's cart in country areas. The first bus service, Shillibeer's Omnibus, began running in 1829 between Paddington and Bank. It ran to a fixed timetable, but carried passengers on demand, successfully taking traffic from both the stage-coach and the hackney carriages. Imitators quickly followed and soon Shillibeer was forced out of business by his competitors. Nevertheless buses spread rapidly so that by the dawn of the motor era most towns, if not adequately served by tramways, had a number of frequent bus services.

In Kent, for example, the Medway Towns were served by routes from New Brompton to Chatham Station, New Brompton to Strood Station and Luton to Strood Hill worked by an association of three operators. At Canterbury the South Eastern and Dover Railway ran a horse bus linking the East and West Stations and a local firm ran a service between the Cricket Ground and St Thomas's Hill. The popular spa resort of Tunbridge Wells hosted several firms, the largest being the Tunbridge Wells, Southborough & District Omnibus Co Ltd, whose routes reached Pembury, Langton and Penshurst.

Longer distance services provided perhaps one or two journeys a day along the main routes, particularly linking those towns without a direct railway line, like Carey's horse bus running from New Romney to Folkestone. Some of these services still retained a stage coach image, and indeed the ability to prebook on inter-urban routes lasted well into motor bus days. Similarly market days in the towns still attracted large gatherings of carriers' vehicles from the more remote villages, with passengers still second to goods.

THE PIONEER MOTOR BUSES

The first motor bus in this country ran in 1897, just a short time after the first practical car had been invented. Kent was not far behind, for in early April 1899 two demonstration motor buses were operated for a week at Tunbridge Wells in connection with a motor show being held in the town.

However the first regular service was operated by Mr E.A. Livet of Canterbury from 24th April 1899, providing a twice-a-day facility to Herne Bay with a Daimler waggonette. In July a twenty seat steam bus was reported in use, possibly borrowed from the Dover & East Kent (see below); the following month the timetable for Canterbury Cricket Week indicated two buses in use, although the service ceased soon after this.

The Dover & East Kent Omnibus Co commenced in early June 1899 working between Dover and St Margaret's-at-Cliffe with a 25 hp Lifu steam bus. (The technology for steam-powered vehicles had been available for many years, and indeed some successful services had run in London and elsewhere in the 1830s; they were forced off the road by high turnpike charges, the notorious 'Red Flag' Act — this required an attendant to walk in front with a red flag, and was not repealed until 1896 — and the odd boiler explosion!) Two further Lifus soon arrived and the service was extended to Deal. These buses were built by the Liquid Fuel & Engineering Co Ltd, Cowes, IOW; a speed of 7 mph on level road was possible and the twin 80-gallon tanks gave 25 miles water supply and 80 miles worth of paraffin fuel. Unfortunately high maintenance costs and bad roads ended the service in 1901.

Also in 1899 Folkestone Motors Ltd began a service to Hythe via Cheriton using a Motor Manufacturing Co of Coventry waggonette;

Red Lion Square, Hythe about 1905; D329 (possibly a Wills') undergoes running repairs, a horse bus awaits custom and a waggonette arrives.

D286 a 1904 MMC waggonette of Wills' of Folkestone carried about ten passengers.
(London Transport)

AN903, one of Autocar's original three ABC double-
deckers stands at Pembury.

operations expanded and their mustard-liveried vehicles reached
Dover in August 1903. A competitor appeared in 1901, when J.W.
Cann began running between Hythe and Folkestone, again with an
MMC. The next firm to enter the fray was E.V. Wills' Folkestone,
Sandgate & Hythe Motor Service, starting in 1903. This ran along
the coast and competed with the horse trams between Hythe and
Sandgate. All three operators continued acquiring more and larger
buses, with both Folkestone Motors and Wills purchasing Maltby
char-a-bancs, locally built at Sandgate.

Further along the South Coast at Hastings a 32-seat Milnes-
Daimler double-decker entered service in March 1903, working
between the Fishmarket and West Marina; this proved successful and
nine others were soon placed on the road on local routes. They were
operated by the Hastings & St Leonards Omnibus Co Ltd, which was
associated with Skinner & Co Ltd, a local horse bus operator, who
also ran three MMC waggonettes and two Daimler char-a-bancs —
these were to become DY17-21 with the arrival of registration
numbers in December 1903.

In July 1906 the Hastings services were acquired by the London
& Westminster Omnibus Co Ltd, trading as Ensign; they sent some
Duncommun double-deckers to join the fleet, which by this time
had added some Durkopp buses. All three makes were of Germanic
origin, although the original fleet was built in England by G.F.
Milnes of Birkenhead (who also built many trams) to a Daimler
design. In April 1907 operations came to an abrupt end when mount-
ing debts caused the firm to go into liquidation and the buses to be

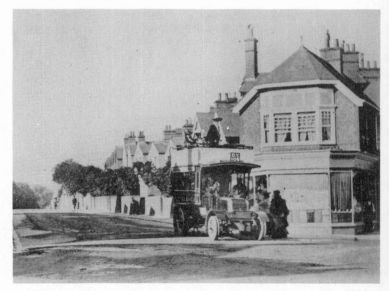

DY106, a Milnes-Daimler double-decker at Silverhill, Hastings circa 1905.

A Dartford-built Hallford, D3206 of Carpenter, Dartford at Farningham circa 1907.
(Pamlin Prints/Dartford Library)

'moonlighted' to London. Ensign's profits had been undermined by the spread of Hastings Tramway Company lines, the first of which had opened in 1905, with the seafront line due to open later in 1907.

At Tunbridge Wells the first regular service was operated by E.M. Tebbs trading as the Tunbridge Wells & District Motor Co running three MMC waggonettes registered D439-41 from the LB&SCR (West) Station to Southborough in competition with the larger horse buses; the first licence was issued in July 1901 and continued until about 1905. By 1904 local comment against the horse buses was increasing, and this prompted the horse bus company to announce in January 1905 it had ordered two Milnes-Daimlers to be fitted with locally-built double-deck bodies; they arrived before Easter and went into service on the Southborough Common to LB&SCR Station road. They were registered D1842/1959, seated 18 on top and 14 inside, and were painted dark green. However they lasted only three months before being sold to a firm at Brighton; the short life at Tunbridge Wells was apparently due to difficulty with a narrow, weak bridge at the SER (Central) Station, which was not rebuilt until 1907. The next appearance of a motor bus service was on 17th September 1908, when W. Oscar Pritchard, trading as Autocar, re-introduced motor working on the Southborough Road. Three vehicles were in service within a month; they were AN903-5, all by the All British Car Co Ltd of Glasgow with bodies seating 17 outside and 18 inside. By January 1910 the loss of traffic to Autocar caused the horse bus firm to go into liquidation, but it was reformed with an injection of local capital as the Tunbridge Wells & Southborough Omnibus Co Ltd, only to fold again in 1912, leaving Autocar the only local operator.

In January 1910 a second route, to Pembury and Lower Green, commenced, covering the loss of the TWS & D horse bus; operations must have been stretched for no new vehicles came until April 1910, when three 32-seat Leylands arrived. The firm also became a limited company in March 1910 and its future seemed assured.

Early operations around Maidstone included the Headcorn, Sutton Valence & Maidstone Omnibus Co Ltd formed in 1904 by W.S. Forster; by about 1908 the service had passed to Captain E. Neve, who traded as Reliance. In the early years a fleet of Clarkson steam buses was operated; they were fitted with well appointed 19-seat saloon bodies and vehicles registered F1247 and D1711 are known. Subsequently Leyland motor buses were used. A competitor came on the scene in 1908 when Kent Motor Services Ltd began running here and also between Faversham and Sittingbourne; demand was over estimated and the 30-seaters were replaced by 12-seaters before operations ceased entirely. A.W. Austen's Commercial Motor Co began with a trial run from Maidstone to London on 27th February 1908 with a hired steam bus. The service began from 9th March, but it was soon switched to run to Chatham and was joined by a Hallford petrol bus. Two more Hallfords were introduced from late June, allowing the return of the steamer, and in July a local service from the Athletic Ground to the North Ward area. Unfortunately they were unable to keep up the hire purchase payments and the buses were repossessed by the makers J. & E. Hall of the Dartford Iron-works; however they kept them running until a purchaser could be

An East Kent & Herne Bay waggonette with tiller steering on the Reculver service.
(M & D and East Kent Bus Club)

found and even extended the service to Gravesend. By 1906 motor buses were in use in the Medway Towns, although here the trams were firmly established.

Another firm to use the Kent-built Hallford was George Humphreys & Co of Sevenoaks, who started working to Westerham on 30th March 1908 and quickly extended to Oxted; five journeys a day were provided.

They were also the obvious choice for J. Carpenter & Son of Dartford, who began a route to Farningham in May 1906 with D3206, later joined by D3881. This was not, however, the first motor bus service along this road as the Dartford & Farningham Motor Bus Co had been running one since the summer of 1904; this operation ceased in 1907. An unusual event took place in June 1909 when D.J. Pitt & Sons began running a competing horse bus over the same route; by the end of that year they had taken over Carpenters and continued to run both horse and motor buses side by side until 1913.

J.W. Gunn of Swanscombe was an early operator, working to Gravesend with a fleet of 16 Scott Stirlings acquired from the London Power Omnibus Co. Over much of the route he was in competition with the trams.

Returning to Herne Bay, the Grand Hotel ran some Daimler wag-gonettes locally during the summer of 1904. At the same time T. Taylor-Strong operated a similar vehicle on short trips with a Sunday journey to Canterbury Cathedral. The following year he was backed by the SE&CR to start a service from Herne Bay Station to Canterbury West with two Panhard waggonettes — one fitted with an ex-horse bus body. This operation was short-lived, but also in 1905 the Automobile Corporation did some demonstration runs on this route with a Thornycroft double-decker in an attempt to attract local investors. This was not forthcoming, but it did encourage the local people to float the East Kent and Herne Bay Motor Omnibus Co Ltd, which commenced in April 1906. This venture failed at the end of 1907 due to lack of cash. The next regular facility on this important route was provided by J.E. West, who began running FO102, an open-sided single-decker, from May 1909.

Further along the coast at Margate, Strong's Garage & Motor Co Ltd introduced a fleet of five Ensign double-deckers in 1910.

D5306, an Ensign belonging to Strong of Margate and new in 1910.
(Dave Bubier Collection)

THE FALSE DAWN OF LONG DISTANCE COACHES

Despite the problems of running these early buses on local routes, some entrepreneurs were soon looking at attacking the longer distance traffic of the railways. J.W. Cann of Folkestone was one such operator and in November 1905 he launched the London & South Coast Motor Service Ltd, registered in London with an authorised capital of £100,000. The prospectus envisaged the operation of fast motor coaches to Margate, Ramsgate, Dover, Folkestone, Hastings and Sheerness, as well as places further afield like Southampton and Oxford. Cann's remaining MMCs were transferred to the new firm and a fleet of new char-a-bancs ordered for 1906 delivery. These were built by the Thames Iron Works, Shipbuilding & Engineering Co Ltd of Greenwich and featured oversized rear wheels with a 50 hp 6 cylinder engine. The first one had only just been delivered when a famous accident shattered the public's confidence in long distance coaching.

In 1905 the London Motor Omnibus Co Ltd (using the fleetname Vanguard) began a service to Brighton using Milnes-Daimler double-deckers. The operation ran reasonably well until 12th July 1906, when the driver of a special journey for a party of part-time firemen from St Mary Cray and Orpington lost control and crashed on Hand-cross Hill in Sussex. At the top of the hill the driver attempted to change down, but the gear box disintegrated — with insufficient braking force, the driver tried to slow the bus by running the wheels along the verge. Unfortunately, an overhanging branch hit the bus, ripping off the upper-deck, pulling the bus into the bank and killing 10 of the passengers.

This accident scuppered a number of similar schemes including those of L&SCM; the few Thames charas that were delivered (Reg Nos D1729/2449/738/9/97/8, FN503/6/14) were used on local work around Folkestone. These machines did prove to be speedy and reliable, no doubt helping to make L&SCM one of the few Edwardian operators to return a steady profit.

One of the London & South Coast Motor Service Ltd Thames char-a-bancs at Hawkhurst on 1st August 1907.

The remains of the Vanguard bus after the Hand-cross Hill accident.

THE FOUNDATIONS OF THE MAJOR COMPANIES

Many of the operations described so far were small affairs, with insufficient capital to expand or even survive; however, there were also a number of entrepreneurs who were backed by the money necessary to grow from a modest start to form the various territorial companies. These were operators that, at an early stage, made agreements with each other over their spheres of influence. At the time these territories were agreed they were often far in excess of the actual network, but they were soon filled by expansions and takeovers. These territories were very important in shaping the industry and allowed the companies to concentrate their resources on competing with the operators within their area, rather than with each other.

The companies and individuals dealt with in this section all had a major role in the formation of the local territorial firms.

BRITISH ELECTRIC TRACTION COMPANY

British Electric Traction Company was a major operator of electric trams across the country, and very soon experimented with motor buses. BET ran a fleet of vehicles in Birmingham from 1906, but they soon fell foul of local bye-laws and were withdrawn by early 1908. Sidney Garcke, son of the BET chairman, took control of six of these buses and brought them to Kent. They all had chassis made by Brush (a BET subsidiary usually making trams) and were overhauled en route, with five (O1284-6/8/91) receiving new slipper bodies, while O1283 obtained a second-hand double-deck body. Under the title of Deal & District Motor Services they commenced operations in April 1908. The initial routes were Deal to St Margaret's Bay and to Kingsdown; by 1910 the former service had been extended to Dover and a new route to Canterbury via Sandwich was also running. In 1912 it became part of British Automobile Traction Co Ltd (a BET subsidiary) with a fleetname of 'British' and a dark green livery. Around this time it had reached Ashford, Hythe and Folkestone and new buses made by Daimler, Leyland, Straker-Squire, and Burford had also arrived.

O1283 the Brush double-decker of Deal & District Motor Services.
(M & D and East Kent Bus Club)

THOMAS TILLING LTD

Thomas Tilling Ltd was a Peckham based horse bus operator, established as early as 1849 and running some 200 vehicles by the turn of the century. The first motor bus ran in 1904, but by this time Thomas Tilling was dead and son Richard and in-laws Thomas and Walter Wolsey were directors. Later Tillings were to operate petrol-electric buses, made at Maidstone by the associated firm of Tilling-Stevens; these vehicles had a conventional petrol engine which drove a dynamo powering an electric motor on the rear axle. A famous route into Kent worked by Tilling was service 47 from Shoreditch to Bromley (1912) and extended to Farnborough the following year.

In 1913 a restrictive agreement was imposed by the London General Omnibus Co, which limited the Tilling fleet in London to 150 buses (later increased to 332, then to 5% of the combined fleets). This prompted Tilling to look to the provinces to expand, and one of the places chosen was Folkestone, where 30 Tilling-Stevens entered service in 1914 under the fleetname of Folkestone District Road Car Co. Despite a number of existing operators plenty of business was found, due to the many troops and refugees in the area at that time.

In late 1911 Wacher & Co Ltd took over West's services between Herne Bay and Canterbury and also introduced a Canterbury to Whitstable route. F.W. Wacher was a Herne Bay coal merchant, who had been running the town's horse buses since 1889, and now had quite a sizeable operation, reaching as far as Sandwich. Subsequently a mixed fleet of motor buses made by Lacre, Commer Car, Daimler, Karrier and Maltby was operated.

O1288 Deal & District Brush saloon at Eastry on the summer-only service to Richborough Castle.

A Lacre bus used on the Herne Bay-Canterbury service; it belonged to Wacher.

(M & D and East Kent Bus Club)

A Folkestone & District Tilling-Stevens (LH8884) at Sandgate, that passed to East Kent on formation. (Pamlin Prints)

LH8880 acquired from Folkestone & District, shows its new East Kent livery as it replenishes its gas-balloon at Canterbury gas works. (East Kent)

Strong's business at Margate was acquired by French, Banister & Co Ltd from April 1912, becoming Margate, Canterbury & District from July 1914 (the French in this concern was Walter Flexman French, who had interests elsewhere as we shall see later). Buses ran to Ramsgate and Canterbury and competing over much of this mileage was George Griggs' Ramsgate Motor Coaches Ltd with routes to Margate and Canterbury. Soon the problems of war resulted in the loss of both staff and vehicles and mutual aid replaced competition to a certain extent. Initially Garcke joined the board of both MC & D and Ramsgate Motor Coaches, with French also joining the latter; after much negotiation this was taken to the logical conclusion with the formation of a new combined company.

THE EAST KENT ROAD CAR COMPANY LTD

On 11th August 1916 the East Kent Road Car Co Ltd was formed with the amalgamation of Folkestone District (28 Tilling-Stevens and a depot at Kent Rd, Cheriton), Deal & District (about 18 buses plus spare bodies and a depot at Albert Rd, Deal), Margate, Canterbury & District (14 buses and a depot at Pleasant Place, Margate), Wacher (9 buses and a depot at High St, Herne Bay) and Ramsgate Motor Coaches (5 buses); an additional garage at Canterbury, Station Road West was also in use, and the Head Office was at 68 Castle Street, Canterbury.

Sidney Garcke was the first chairman, and he remained on the board of East Kent until his death in 1948. Other board members included French, Wacher and Griggs, with Thomas and Walter Wolsey representing the Tilling interest.

There is some doubt as to the exact fleet on formation due to conflicting and incomplete records, although this can be partially explained by some chassis carrying lorry bodies or without bodies. Seventy-two is the officially quoted figure; many were in poor condition and, despite the delivery of some new buses that had been ordered by the constituent operators, only forty buses were in running order by the end of 1916. Other problems of wartime operation meant that women road staff had to be employed, and the shortage of petrol resulted in some buses being converted to run on town gas from a large balloon fitted to the roof. A further restriction was the Local Government (Emergency Provisions) Act, 1916; this forbade new routes except with the consent of the Highway Authorities concerned. In Kent authority could only be obtained on payment of £10 per route mile per annum, or up to 1d per bus mile, whichever was the greater.

In 1917 three unidentified machines were acquired from Joseph Jackson (Westgate-on-Sea) Ltd, and three secondhand buses obtained in 1918 were to be the only relief on the vehicle side until the end of hostilities, but East Kent were exceptionally well placed to take a leading role in the post-war expansion.

Another vehicle that was part of East Kent's initial fleet was this Commer Car (KT2152), new to Wacher, Herne Bay in 1914.

WALTER FRENCH

Walter Flexman French began in the transport business in 1881 as a bicycle manufacturer, but he was to become a most influential pioneer in the bus industry, not only in Kent but over much of South-East England. His first endeavour in this field was in 1899, when two Daimler waggonettes were purchased to operate between Piccadilly and Putney. This was soon abandoned, but in 1901 seven MMC waggonettes were working from Clapham to Streatham as the South Western Motor Car Co Ltd. In 1904 he left London for a few years to run the Sussex Motor Road Car Co Ltd, at Worthing. Two years later he returned to London as the agent for the Ryknield Motor Co, soon after setting up French's Ltd (Motor Jobmasters) — later becoming French's Garage & Motor Works Ltd — with a fleet of Ryknield buses.

In May 1910 he bought the bus service between Maidstone and Gravesend from Hall's of Dartford, who had operated it since repossessing the vehicles from the Commercial Motor Co. French altered the title to the Maidstone, Chatham, Gravesend & District Omnibus Service, and gave the day-to-day control of the firm to his son George Flexman French. This allowed Walter to concentrate on other ventures elsewhere, including at Aldershot (1912) and Guildford (1914).

The forerunner of M & D was the Commercial Motor Co; one of their Hallford double-deckers at Rose Yard Mews, Maidstone, probably on 9th May 1908 — the first day of the Chatham service. (M & D and East Kent Bus Club)

KT6415 a 1915 Straker-Squire of M & D.   (M & D and East Kent Bus Club)

THE MAIDSTONE & DISTRICT MOTOR SERVICES LTD

On 22nd March 1911 this operation was reformed into a limited company as The Maidstone & District Motor Services Ltd, with the local Col. H.I. Robinson joining the Frenches in the enterprise, which had an initial capital of £4,000.

At this stage the fleet consisted of five Hallfords dating from 1908/9; D4501 with a 24-seat char-a-banc body and D3449/3944/ 4465/4608 with open-top double-deck bodies. They operated routes to Gravesend and West Malling from a yard at St Peter's Street, Maidstone. One interesting feature of the early years was the carriage of goods at night; the buses were built with easily detachable bodies, which were removed each night and lorry bodies fitted. During the night fruit for Covent Garden, hops for the London factors, or toffees from the nearby Sharp's factory were conveyed, and next morning the bus bodies were remounted for another day's passenger use. In 1911 two single-deck Hallfords were delivered (D6490/ 6585), followed by two more the next year (D7896/8650); these were the last of this make purchased, the 1913 intake being the first of many Daimler and Tilling-Stevens to join the fleet. Route expansion continued with a Rochester via Burham service in 1911 and M & D began competing with Neve on the Sutton Valence run from 1912.

In 1913 BET, through its bus subsidiary BAT, took an interest in the firm, with Sidney Garcke joining the board. The influx of BET capital now available no doubt helped the rapid expansion that took place before the Great War. By 1914 the fleet strength had increased to 21, with a new depot in Upper Stone Street, Maidstone and new routes running to Sevenoaks, Faversham, Ashford, Tenterden and Hastings via Hawkhurst; an additional route ran from Chatham to Faversham. To work these routes buses were based at a number of places, including Cranbrook, Faversham, Sevenoaks, Hastings and Gillingham. The war, particularly the problem of finding new buses, caused a lull in this growth, so the 1915 fleet intake included a varied selection of makes like Caledon, Commer, Ensign and Romar that lasted but a short time in the fleet. More successful were three

B5531 a 1916 Leyland of Neve, Sutton Valence, in Church St, Maidstone.
(Julian Brown Collection)

Straker-Squires that worked the Maidstone to Chatham service; four more of this make were diverted to Bournemouth & District (another French fleet) only to be requisitioned and sent to Mesopotamia! In 1916 Neve sold out to M & D, becoming depot supervisor at Hastings. With this acquisition M & D became the sole operator on the Tenterden road, and three Leyland single-deckers were added to the fleet — two of which (B5531/788) were only six months old. Only one new bus arrived in 1916, with none at all in the next two years. Maintaining operations became increasingly difficult towards the end of the war, and several routes were suspended, including Maidstone to Rochester via Burham.

The first bus owned by Standen was this Dennis, KT937 seen at Newington.

Standing at Minster is KT7608 a Daimler new to Sheerness and District, but part of the Sheppey Motor Transport fleet when this photo was taken.

STANDEN AND SHEPPEY MOTOR TRANSPORT

T. Standen & Sons of Sittingbourne began operating in October 1913 with KT937/88, both built by Dennis, and further buses of this make followed quickly. One early route was from Sittingbourne to Rainham; some buses were also sent to Sheerness, where they began a local service competing with the trams of the Sheerness and District Electrical Power and Traction Co — a BET subsidiary. This small system opened in 1903 running from a depot at Sheerness East to Cheyney Rock and the Dockyard; proposed lines to Queenborough and Minster were never built, mainly due to opposition from the Sheppey Light Railway. This system was unique in Britain in using the German Siemens bow-collectors.

The Standen route ran as a circular serving Sheerness and Queenborough, working one way via the Dockyard and the other way via Sheerness East and Halfway. This cut deeply into the tramway's already slim revenue and to compete the tramway company obtained three unidentified Daimler buses to run on the same route. By 1914 Standen also ran to Minster and Eastchurch and between Sheerness and Sittingbourne (with a 2/- toll to cross the Kingsferry Bridge); the Sheerness based fleet was 6 single-deckers at this stage. Two more Daimlers EO578/9 joined the S & D fleet in 1915, being transferred from the BAT operation at Barrow. With a sizeable operating loss and problems in obtaining spares for the German electrical equipment it became the first British electric tramway system to be replaced by buses, closing on 7th July 1917. Competition continued only

until 21st July when S & D and Standen's Sheppey fleets merged to become the Sheppey Motor Transport Co Ltd to the advantage of both operators, and of the general public who complained that the competition had led to the timetable being forgotten!

Initially the fleet contained three Dennises from Standen and four Daimlers from S & D, with some second-hand Daimlers coming from M & D. The close association of Standen with BET at Sheerness seems to have allowed their Sittingbourne area operations to escape heavy competition from M & D, who merely passed through on the way to Faversham, although Standens bought out the BET interest in SMT by 1923. This was not the end of competition on Sheppey as Grimer's Enterprise Motor Services was active by 1926; it entered a working agreement with M & D in 1928, and was fully absorbed in December 1930.

With the approach of the Road Traffic Act, Standen's, like many smaller firms, decided to leave the industry to concentrate on other interests; accordingly M & D took over both SMT (with 22 buses and the former tram depot) and the Standen fleet at Sittingbourne (nine buses) from 8th January 1930. Mr Arthur Standen (one of the original 'Sons') was recently still alive although well into his nineties; still a BET shareholder from the takeover in 1930, he showed me a silver cigarette-case presented to him for driving a char-a-banc from Sheerness to the 1914 Epsom Derby and also loaned the two photos reproduced here.

This North Kent Daimler (LH8989) was working on the Chatham-West Malling route when photographed at Snodland.

NORTH KENT MOTOR SERVICES

Another local tramway to operate motor buses was the Gravesend & Northfleet Electric Tramway Co. Using the fleetname of North Kent Motor Services, they commenced running in 1913. This firm was also a member of the BET group, and as such was closely associated with M & D; initial services were to Dartford and Chatham, the latter being to all intents a joint service with M & D. North Kent's route F ran Chatham to West Malling (apparently Saturday and Sunday only), well into M & D territory; this route later became M & D 20. Daimlers were the original choice of vehicle, but like other companies they were forced to acquire different makes during the war years and in 1915 they took delivery of two Burfords and four or five Belsizes; at this time the fleet was quoted as also containing eight Daimlers and two LGOC B types.

In 1920 the bus fleet passed to M & D, 15th March being the date the financial arrangements were completed. However, there was little physical change as the buses were already painted green and they continued to park at a small depot adjoining the Northfleet tram shed.

EAST SURREY TRACTION CO LTD

East Surrey was the brainchild of Arthur Hawkins and it started by running two motor buses between Reigate and Redhill on 23rd May 1911. By 1914 nine dark blue buses were plying on various routes around Redhill and Dorking from a depot in Bell Street, Reigate.

East Surrey arrived in Kent on 11th April 1914, when the Reigate to Godstone Green service was extended via Oxted, Westerham, and Chipstead to Riverhead. Sevenoaks was the ultimate target, but the council were slow to issue the licence for the service. To force the pace, the route was extended to terminate on private ground at Tubs Hill Station from 17th April. Mr G. Humphrey, the existing operator

between Oxted and Sevenoaks, expressed his concern at this competition, and when East Surrey announced they would run a bus ahead of his service from 8th June, he withdrew without a fight. With the necessary licence finally issued the service reached the Market Place from 17th June; it ran every two hours and was worked by three new Daimlers (P5350/73/87) fitted with second-hand double-deck bodies. Because of a low bridge at Oxted upper-deck passengers had to alight while the bus passed under.

In 1914 East Surrey made two important territorial agreements, one with London General and the other with M & D. At this time LGOC was expanding rapidly towards the (then) country towns around London; although the agreement concerned only the Reigate area it was to herald one of wider scope in 1921. The agreement with M & D, who also reached Sevenoaks in 1914, set the boundary as the road to Dartford, somewhat anticipating future growth. On 7th July 1921, following over a year of discussions, East Surrey and LGOC signed a complex document which resulted in East Surrey developing the area outside the Metropolitan Police boundary as LGOCs agents. Basically LGOC provided the capital, with East Surrey paying a fixed mileage charge plus a share of the profits. LGOC supplied many buses, both new and second-hand, made by Associated Equipment Company (AEC), an LGOC offshoot; as a result LGOC red was adopted from 1922.

Another territorial arrangement was made in 1921 with Autocar of Tunbridge Wells, which resulted in East Surrey taking over Autocar's long route to Farnborough north of Sevenoaks with effect from 26th May 1921. For this service three ex-LGOC AEC B types were acquired and based at the Railway Hotel, Bat & Ball Station. From 13th August 1921 this route was extended to Bromley North Station and numbered S2. A week later S2B commenced between Farnborough and Sidcup via Orpington and the Cray Valley, and three new routes started from West Croydon; these were S3 to Sevenoaks, S4 to Edenbridge and S5 to Reigate. A low bridge at South Croydon caused both S3 & S4 to be operated by ex-War Department AECs

Dunton Green depot with a line of ex-LGOC AEC B-types still carrying LGOC fleet numbers.
(London Transport)

PC9250 East Surrey 79, another B-type, but supplied new, at Uckfield in 1923 at the end of the long route from Croydon. (Pamlin Prints)

fitted with new single-deck bodies. Both ran every two hours on a common route via Chelsham, splitting at Botley Hill then via Westerham (S3) or Limpsfield (S4); one bus was based at Bat & Ball, with the rest at Oxted.

Expansion was now rapid, with S7 Sidcup-Dartford-Swanley-Crockenhill starting in April 1922 from an outstation at Swanley Junction. In the same month a permanent depot was opened at Dunton Green to replace the open-air yard at Bat & Ball. June of that year saw the start of S10 Bromley North-Biggin Hill-Westerham-Reigate, with three buses outbased at Westerham. S10 replaced LGOC 36 to Westerham Hill, although Sunday operation continued to Westerham until the end of the Summer season and to Westerham Hill until 1923.

From 1st September 1922 S1 Dartford-Sevenoaks was operated, replacing the Allen service; it had an half-hourly frequency north of Farningham, but only four buses a day to Sevenoaks. In May 1924 this was increased to hourly and at the same time extended to Bexley (then Bexleyheath four months later), competing with the Bexley UDC trams. Other notable changes in 1924 included the extension of S4 from Edenbridge to East Grinstead, S7 becoming a circular — returning to Sidcup via St Mary Cray — and S3 was converted to double-deck on being diverted away from the low bridge.

Late in 1924 a route numbering system for London, controlled by the police, resulted in East Surrey's routes being renumbered, normally by the addition of 400 to the previous S-number, although S2B became 411 — many of these numbers are still recognisable today.

Key events in 1925 were the opening of more new depots, replacing various outstations; these were at Godstone, East Grinstead and Swanley Junction, where the yard of the Lullingstone Castle pub had long been outgrown. On the service front the return loop on 407 (ex S7), was diverted at St Mary Cray to Orpington and Bromley.

East Surrey's Swanley Junction Depot. (London Transport)

The 1926 summer timetable saw the doubling of buses on 410 and 403, and as a result S24 Reigate-Sevenoaks was withdrawn, thus ending East Surrey's original link with Kent; there has never been a service between these towns since then, but connections could be made at Westerham. In later days it did allow the special lowbridge double-deckers required to work 410, due to the bridge at Oxted, to be concentrated at Godstone. On the negative side 404 was cut back to Tatsfield and then with the winter timetable to Oxted leaving only the southern section to East Grinstead still running.

Above: FN4460, a 1920 Thornycroft char-a-banc of the Isle of Thanet Motor
Co Ltd, at the Bell Inn, Minster. It later passed to East Kent.

Below: Showing its Silver Queen fleetnames, this Thornycroft char-a-bus was
one of three to pass to East Kent in 1925; it is seen at Margate Harbour.

12

A joint service with Autocar of Tunbridge Wells commenced on 26th January 1927; this was 24 Horley-East Grinstead-Hartfield-Tunbridge Wells and it replaced separate services that previously met at Hartfield. Autocar supplied two 30-seat AEC Y-types, with East Surrey using three 20-seat AEC 202s. From 31st October 1928 24 was extended to Reigate, making use of the extensive layover time in the original timetable. Another new route to appear was 30 East Grinstead-Cowden, which started on 26th March 1927 using a 16-seat Garford; it was extended to Edenbridge the next year. It was further extended to Westerham and Caterham in January 1929, partially replacing two very short-lived operations; 32 between Westerham and Uckfield and 33 Caterham to Westerham Hill. This arrangement lasted only two months before the Kent section of 30 was withdrawn and 28 East Grinstead to Dormansland was projected to Edenbridge and Westerham, with East Grinstead to Cowden passing to J. Sargent's East Grinstead Motor Services.

Returning to North Kent, the 1928 summer service showed 407 cut back to Orpington Station, but 411 was doubled to give an half-hourly headway along the Cray Valley, and maintain the frequency between Orpington and Bromley. New route 25 Dartford-Wilmington-Stanhill commenced in January 1929, with one bus from Swanley Junction; it was extended to Birchwood the following October, where it connected with LGOC 21 (City-Lewisham-Sidcup-Farningham).

Depot extensions were made at Dunton Green in 1930 and Swanley Junction in 1931 to house the ever increasing fleet.

From 1st April 1931 LGOC decided to transfer two routes worked from a small depot at Crayford; these were 99c Erith-Crayford-Dartford and 199a Erith-Dartford direct. Service 99 first reached Dartford from Woolwich in 1922 and was split at Erith in 1926. The depot at Crayford was beyond a low-bridge which would not allow closed-top double-deckers to enter; just prior to East Surrey's takeover LGOC had replaced the open-top NS-types with five AEC Regal T class saloons, which passed to East Surrey.

The last new East Surrey route in Kent was 422 from Orpington to Eltham Well Hall via Petts Wood, which commenced on 7th October 1931 with Swanley based AEC Regals.

From 12th June 1929 East Surrey became a full LGOC subsidiary, after many years of close association. East Surrey was wound up from 20th January 1932, when it was merged with the National Omnibus and Transport Co Ltd, which had enjoyed a similar position north of the Thames, to become the London General Country Services Ltd. A green livery was adopted as standard by this new subsidiary, which was carried on by the country department of London Transport in 1933.

A Guy saloon at Folkestone with South Coast Motor Services fleetnames, although the fleet was by this stage under East Kent control.
(M & D and East Kent Bus Club)

WILLIAM ALLEN'S COMPANIES

Another person to play a leading role in the formation of the industry was William Percy Allen; from an office in Rochester Row, Westminster he ran bus services in many areas. The Allen Omnibus Co Ltd ran a fleet of yellow Straker-Squire double-deckers on the streets of London from 1913 to November 1916 when, together with the associated Premier fleet, they were the last major obstacle at that time to LGOC supremacy. Subsequently he operated buses (often under the Silver Queen fleetname) at Clacton and Canvey Island and in Worcestershire and Lincolnshire; the latter was the forerunner of the Lincolnshire Road Car Co Ltd, a fleet that Allen was to be chairman of in later years. In Kent Allen began at Farningham on 19th July 1913, when he replaced Pitt's workings to Dartford, which seem to have ceased a few weeks earlier. A second route from Dartford to Northfleet lasted only a few weeks, as no licences were issued, but from 8th October a service from Dartford to Swanley Junction by way of Hextable commenced; at this stage the Farningham fleet is recorded as being four double-deckers and one char-a-banc, all Straker-Squires.

Before the Great War operations had also begun between Sittingbourne and Greenstreet, Strood and Rainham, at Ramsgate (by April 1914 as the Isle of Thanet Motor Co Ltd, later using the Silver Queen name) and at Folkestone from April 1914 (again using the Silver Queen fleetname). Although the first two soon ceased in favour of other operators, Allen's position in Folkestone was strengthened by the rescue of the London & South Coast fleet which had gone into liquidation. This was reformed by Allen as the London & South Coast Motor Services (1915) Ltd and continued to run as a separate fleet.

Returning to the Farningham based venture, the Dartford-Swanley bus was withdrawn in 1915, following several suspensions due to operating problems, especially the poor roads. However the main route, which ran roughly every two hours, was extended to Sevenoaks three times a day from 8th January 1917 replacing the local trains via Otford, which were suspended as a wartime economy measure. In late 1918 Allen acquired eight Leyland double-deckers from LGOC, permitting hourly working north of Farningham, the restoration of the Swanley route and a new facility to Longfield from Dartford. Just as Allen had been forced to leave London in 1916, he was forced out of this area by the expanding M & D and East Surrey concerns. The Swanley route lapsed again in 1921, and the Longfield route passed to M & D (service 27) from 14th January 1922. Despite agreeing some years before to transfer the Sevenoaks route to East Surrey, this move finally took place on 1st September 1922.

After the war the two Folkestone based fleets were housed in a former airship hangar at Capel; as well as local excursions, bus services were run from Folkestone to Hythe, Shorncliffe Camp via Cheriton, and Dover. Thanet operations included routes from Ramsgate to Sandwich and to Margate via Broadstairs or Westwood. Allen sold his Thanet operation to East Kent on 1st August 1925, together with four Thornycroft buses. Although Allen became an East Kent director from December 1925, operations at Folkestone continued and indeed were increased by the arrival of at least three char-a-bancs from Thanet. Ten Silver Queen vehicles passed to East Kent control in 1926, but the final takeover proved to be protracted, especially as it was part of a much larger scheme; the agreement was eventually signed on 1st December 1928. Nevertheless, it was not until 30th November 1933 that the L&SCMS (1915) Ltd fleet was finally absorbed, and in fact it was also given control of the other operations acquired by East Kent during this era. Allen remained an East Kent director until 1959.

Typical of the vehicles used by the smaller operator, this Crossley with about 14 seats ran with Garnett of Herne Bay; this firm sold out to East Kent in 1935.

A general view of Margate at the height of the era of competition.

This 1925 Morris had a fourteen-seat body built by East Kent. The driver poses by his bus on a rural route near Dover. (M & D and East Kent Bus Club)

THE ERA OF COMPETITION

The period after the First World War until the introduction of the Road Traffic Act of 1930 was one of rapid expansion and hectic competition. During the war there had been many improvements to vehicle design and reliability and vast numbers of lorries and ambulances were built for the War Department. After the war these vehicles were gradually released to civilian use and many chassis were refurbished and rebodied as buses or char-a-bancs. East Kent made some use of this source, but for the many small operators who started during these years it was a cheap means of getting a bus.

Also popular with the minor operators were the extended car chassis, which could be fitted with bodies seating around fourteen people. Vehicles seating twenty or less did not require a conductor and were therefore cheap to buy and run. As an extra bonus full-sized buses were restricted to 12 mph, but vehicles less than 30 cwt could go at 20 mph; thus they were useful for poaching traffic from the major operators, using the higher speed to overtake between stops. In order to play them at their own game both East Kent and M & D bought buses of this type, which were known as 'chasers'; East Surrey also put to good use some of these that were acquired on taking over other firms. From 1928 the speed for all vehicles on pneumatic tyres was increased to 20 mph, thus reducing this particular advantage.

These small buses were also well used by the country carrier type operator, and permitted the development of some incredibly tenuous, and in many cases short-lived rural links, like Red Road Car's service from Maidstone to Hollingbourne via Detling and the Pilgrim's Way.

14

A tramway company's Leyland stands at Birchington Square with a competing bus behind, possibly a Sayer's Thornycroft.

Two later Isle of Thanet Tramway buses, a Thornycroft for the narrow roads on route 5, with an ex-Lanarkshire Daimler behind.

(M & D and East Kent Bus Club)

Early buses were mainly used by the professional middle class, as they were too dear for the working class to afford, except for the occasional trip to the country or sea-side. For this reason few services started before 0900, and many ran with a reduced frequency until lunch time, then continued until quite late at night.

By 1922 routes began to gain early morning timings (not Sundays) to cater for regular work journeys; M & D operated some early Monday only trips into Gillingham, presumably for workers who took lodgings during the week. Cheaper, more reliable buses, the arrival of pneumatic tyres (rubber was very dear at this time) and competition reduced fares. This, coupled with increased living standards and worker mobility, meant that most people could afford to use buses, and by 1930 many villages had a 'before 0900 arrival' bus to the nearest town, with trunk and town routes starting at six or seven. Many routes also had a late bus at least one day a week, which waited for the end of the theatre performance. Saturday afternoons and Summer Sundays were still the peak times, with long queues and countless reliefs on routes like Canterbury to Margate.

Drivers' hours regulations were non-existent and staff would often be at the wheel for twelve or even fourteen hours a day and then prepare their bus for the next day's work! This was the price of survival during these days of intense rivalry; and it is not surprising that the Government decided that greater legal control was needed to end this stage of the bus industry.

Let us now look at some specific examples of fierce competition in this area.

COMPETITION IN THANET – TRAMS VERSUS BUSES

The Isle of Thanet Electric Tramway & Lighting Co Ltd opened the first section of their line in April 1901; the trams were eventually to run from Westbrook via Margate, Cliftonville, Broadstairs, Ramsgate Harbour to Ramsgate Town Station. It was part of the British Thomson-Houston group and, like many tramway companies, it also supplied the area with electricity from its generating plant.

Initially the many horse-brake operators lost business and there were a few angry clashes, but they soon found other work, especially in the lucrative summer months. Indeed within ten years it was the trams that were suffering at the hands of the new motor buses and Isle of Thanet decided in 1913 to run their own buses, with four single-deckers arriving that year: R17 a Straker-Squire, a Dennis (registration unknown), a Tilling-Stevens FR1923, and a Leyland KT232.

They were put to use serving the small town of Birchington to the west of Margate, not reached by the tramway, and this was taken advantage of by several bus operators. This in turn reduced traffic on the Westbrook section of the line, which the tram company were keen to counter. At one stage a feeder bus was run from Birchington Square to connect with the trams at Westbrook, but this failed to attract enough passengers and through workings to Margate were introduced.

One of the early operators over this road was the Margate, Canterbury & District which, as already mentioned, was to become a founder

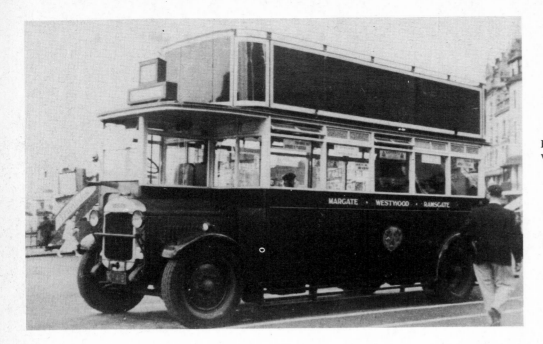

KP419, a Thornycroft open-topper of 1928, working on the Margate-Ramsgate direct service.
(M & D and East Kent Bus Club)

An East Kent Tilling-Stevens with petrol-electric transmission stands at the Wood Avenue terminus about 1930. (M & D and East Kent Bus Club)

member of East Kent in 1916. Another firm to work this route was W.H. Walker of Birchington (trading as Birchingtonia), who was in business by at least January 1915 when KT4102, a 40 hp McCurd, arrived. This was soon followed by KT4381 – a Leyland – and the next year by KT7853, a Straker-Squire. The firm survived until 1929 before it was acquired by East Kent; financial control was from 1st May, but it was not until at least October that the physical takeover of the buses took place, although the Thornycroft double-decker and four single-deckers were soon replaced by standard East Kent buses.

Not all operators lasted so long; W. Sayer & Sons of Margate placed two brand new double-deck Thornycrofts on this service in early 1919, but they lasted only a few months, selling out to East Kent at the end of the summer. Also competing on this road were West Margate Coaches, whose fleet included some former LGOC B types. They sold out in 1921, this time to the tram company, who took over two B types LF8832, LH8277, and two AEC single-deckers KE4726/6838.

Other routes to experience heavy competition were the direct route from Margate to Ramsgate via Westwood and, despite tram cars running every couple of minutes, on the Margate-Broadstairs-Ramsgate route, although the bus routes used alternative roads at various places. Both of these routes were worked by East Kent and Allen's Silver Queen fleet, with Isle of Thanet buses also working on the direct route. This was the province of four 50-seat open-top

double-decker Thornycrofts delivered in 1919, two of which were reconditioned ex-WD chassis. Thornycrofts remained the choice for new vehicles until the first Daimlers arrived in 1929. In 1926 three small Berliets were acquired with the business of Carlton Coaches of Garlinge.

By 1928 the Isle of Thanet routes were:
1 Margate Harbour-Westgate-Birchington Station.
2 Margate Harbour-Westwood-Ramsgate Harbour.
3 'Thanet Circular'. Margate-Birchington-Minster-Pegwell-Ramsgate-Broadstairs-Margate.
4 Garlinge-Margate-Dane Valley (Millmead Road).
5 Margate Station-Cliftonville then via Kingsgate or Reading Street or St Peter's Street to Broadstairs.
6 Margate Harbour-St Peter's-Broadstairs-Ramsgate Harbour.
7 Palm Bay-Margate-Garlinge.
8 Newington-St Lawrence-Ramsgate Harbour.
 This route, despite fierce competition elsewhere, was joint with East Kent, but Isle of Thanet ceased to participate on this route in 1932.
10 Palm Bay-Margate-Westgate Bay Avenue.
 In the late twenties competition between the two main companies intensified, and in 1927 the tram company's bus fleet adopted an emerald green livery (the trams using a brighter shade of red from the same time) to emphasise the distinction from East Kent. The fleet was strengthened in 1930 by the arrival of a large batch of

KT2225 an MMC of Wills of Folkestone, in Tontine Street, Folkestone on a women's outing.

Daimler single-deckers obtained from Lanarkshire Transport; these were to help the increased frequency being operated on a number of routes.

There were also many small operators in this area, some just poaching traffic from the main companies in the summer months on the main bus routes; others looked to the important excursion traffic to make a living. A few, like Blue Rambler Coaches, evolved into the modern independents, concentrating on private hire and contract work, but many fell by the way-side, including the following firms who were bought out by East Kent:

G.F. Darr (Alexandre Coaches) Broadstairs — from 1st August 1928, with four small coaches, after some five years of operation.

R.E. Hodgman of Ramsgate — in November 1928, with one vehicle.

S.H. Tobin (Unique) of Margate — on 5th January 1930; they were running buses by 1923, with four Lancias and two Unics, all twenty-seaters, passing to East Kent.

Even so there were a number of important firms who survived into the next era, and the story of their demise is covered later.

FOLKESTONE

Further round the Kent Coast at Folkestone rival proprietors were also fighting for business; the skill of the driver in beating the opposition to the passengers waiting at stops en route is shown by this well-known quote by a conductor from this era, which was published in the East Kent staff magazine:

"We had a bad day. The takings were poor. Arrived in the garage about 10.30 pm, the 'Old Man' asked Charlie 'How were things today?' Charlie replied 'What d'yer expect with a fool like that behind the steerin' wheel? He knows nothing about bussin' and strikes me he never will. All he thinks about is gettin' 'is gears nice and being perlite to everbody. 'E says it isn't right to keep to the middle of the road to 'old the opposition back. I do'an want 'im no more!' — He never 'ad me no more! Those were the days!"

The main companies working here — East Kent, Folkestone Motors, Wills' Pullman Coaches, and Allen's two fleets, Silver Queen and London & South Coast — have already been discussed, but in addition there were many small firms, often owner-drivers with just one vehicle. Once again it is a story of the bigger operators gradually obtaining supremacy at the expense of the smaller businesses.

By 1921 some of these one-man-bands had amalgamated to form the Co-operative Travel Services Ltd — known as Co-Operbangs — which was running to Deal via Dover with a fleet of buses with sunshine roofs and on local excursions with char-a-bancs.

Folkestone Motors sold out to its old rival, Wills, in 1926 and they in turn passed to East Kent the next year, along with seven char-a-bancs. Also in 1927 the Bourne's Garage fleet of F. Macklin (one bus and three charas) was acquired by East Kent.

On 1st December 1928, after protracted negotiations, East Kent took control of the bulk of the competition when the 'Co-Operbangs' went under the control of the L&SCMS fleet (Allen by this time was an East Kent director), which continued as an associated company. In 1930 some vehicles that East Kent had acquired from Cambrian Coaching were allocated to this fleet, which was finally absorbed from 30th November 1933, contributing thirty buses to the main fleet.

In the three years following this takeover, East Kent also acquired ten other firms in the Folkestone area; the majority were one vehicle concerns, but two were more substantial. They were Partridge of Alkham with four small buses, who capitulated in October 1929 after East Kent had started a Folkestone-Alkham-Dover service two months earlier on 1st August, and Hunt & Russell of Hawkinge with five vehicles in 1930.

Much of the competition was centred on three intensive routes to Hythe, Dover and Shorncliffe. The buses on the Hythe route ensured the end of the horse trams between Hythe and Sandgate after September 1921, although they had only run during the summer since resuming after war-time suspension. The 1929 East Kent timetable shows a bus every two minutes on this route, which split after the Town Centre, to serve residential areas at Wood Avenue, or ran to the Junction Station; by the summer of 1935 (when East Kent were the sole operator) there were forty-four buses an hour! All the major firms worked this road, and also the local route via Cheriton to the army camp at Shorncliffe. Even with a virtual monopoly there was a bus every three minutes (six before 10.00). The Dover Road, being rather rural beyond Capel, only attracted East Kent, Allen and the Co-Operative of the major firms, with a headway of every eight minutes being provided once East Kent had gained control.

Standing at Hastings Station in this 1926 view is DY3745, a Skinner's Leyland working the Ore route. (Pamlin Prints)

The majority of Hastings trolleybuses were these Guy single-deckers; this one is seen in war-time condition at Silverhill depot.
(M & D and East Kent Bus Club)

Eight Hastings trolleybuses were open-top double-deckers; 7 (DY4969) is shown here decorated from the 1934 Carnival.

COLOURFUL HASTINGS

Around 1930 buses of all colours were working services in the Hastings area, but within five years many of these had gone; of the major operators M & D buses were dark green, with Southdown favouring a much lighter shade, East Kent vehicles were a rich red, with Timpson's using cream and Skinner dark blue; the new trolley buses (trackless trams) of Hastings & District were maroon. The following poem reproduced from 'The Green 'Un' — the M & D staff magazine — of August 1930 helps to recreate the scene:

THE SEA FRONT SERVICE

Lions and Tillings and S.G. Elevens,
Leave every Morris and poor Austin
    Sevens,
They cane poor old Timpson and
    worry poor Skinner,
And the Trackless, I'm sure,
    get thinner and thinner.

Down London Road,
Comes a char-a-banc load,
By the rattle and roar
It's a Battle car, sure,
Yes, 169 with her rad. to the fore!

Now just wait a tick,
It's the Northiam click,
Westfield combines,
Driver watch those signs.

Up goes the green,
Oh it's a scream,
To watch our Front service
Glide o'er the surface,
To Wellington Square.

Skinner, the former horse bus operator, had introduced motor vehicles before the Great War, although several double-deckers were quickly requisitioned. Five new Leyland open-toppers were delivered between 1925 and 1927 and worked a service from Hastings Station to Ore via the Old Town.

Timpson's, a London based operator with a coach service to Hastings, became involved in local services in 1927 with the purchase of West Hill Services, which had run from Priory Road to Manor Road since at least 1924. A shed was built at Clegg Street adjoining the M & D depot, with a fleet of some twenty-six buses. The Skinner bus fleet and workings were acquired in April 1933, but in turn Timpson's sold out to M & D from 3rd March 1934, with sixty-four buses changing hands. The old Skinner route became service 27, Bulverhythe-Memorial-Fairlight Glen/St Helens became 44/a; new 71 was Memorial-The Briars, 72 Downs Rd-Memorial-The Briars, 73 Circular via Silverhill-Harrow Inn-St Helens, 74 Priory Ave-Memorial-St Leonards, 75 Manor Rd-Memorial-Wishing Tree-Crowhurst and 76 Memorial-St Johns Church-Silverhill. Routes to Pett and Pett Level via Fairlight Cove were transferred to East Kent (later numbered 127/8) as this fell within their agreed territory after East Kent's arrival from the Rye direction in 1920.

Southdown Motor Services Ltd, the major operator in the rest of Sussex, only arrived here on joint operations from Eastbourne, and the South Coast Express, which was evolving about 1930, is a story in itself.

The Hastings Tramway Co began the introduction of trolleybuses on 1st April 1928, with the last tram running on 15th May 1929. The new fleet consisted of fifty single-deckers and eight unique open-top double-deckers with the fleetname 'Hastings & District'. The system was the least intensively operated of all the British networks, particularly on the rural circular route via The Ridge, which only ran every forty minutes.

Almost everywhere the trolleys were subject to intense bus competition, so it was hardly unexpected when they also sold out to M & D; this took effect from 11th November 1935. The vehicles were repainted into green and cream with Hastings Tramway fleetnames and the undertaking retained as a subsidiary.

Number 9 in the Dengate fleet was NJ2176, a 1933 Bedford WLB with a Thurgood body, here seen on the Rye-Hawkhurst service.
(M & D and East Kent Bus Club)

SOME RURAL BATTLES

Even the thinly populated rural roads attracted competing firms. Hastings was served by several firms from its hinterland ('Northiam click and Westfield combines'), with Dengate of Beckley and Northiam being an important firm whose history is dealt with in greater detail later. Dengate was also involved on the Rye to Hawkhurst road, which was also served by M & D and Weald of Kent at varying stages. M & D was probably first on this route with service 30 (Hawkhurst-Rye-Brede-Hastings) in operation from June 1922 using a bus based at Northiam. This was later split at Rye, with the Hawkhurst leg becoming 31. By 1929 it seems that Weald of Kent had been running on this road for some time; at this stage Dengate appeared on this route, and the M & D 1929 timetable shows route 31 as suspended (but a Northiam based bus continued to work to Rye for service 30), although the reason for this apparent surrender is not known. The road was not intensely worked with each operator running only a

few journeys a day and, later accepting each other's return tickets. M & D's route 31 stayed suspended until 1st November 1933, when Weald of Kent was taken over.

Further north the rural roads around Maidstone were also subject to some rivalry between Red Road Cars, Buck's Motor Services and M & D.

Buck's, of Week Street, Maidstone, were in business by 1921 and, in 1928 became a subsidiary of the London based firm of Cambrian, who also had a number of coach services in Kent. In November 1929 the entire Cambrian operation in Kent was jointly acquired by M & D and East Kent and by this stage the Buck's fleet had grown to eighteen vehicles wearing a grey livery. The final timetable showed these routes; to Chart Sutton via Boughton (daily), to Coxheath (daily), Leeds circular via Langley and Bearsted Yeoman (daily), Bearsted circular via Penenden Heath and Yeoman (daily), to Ulcombe via

KL2499 a 1924 Vulcan of Buck's of Maidstone standing at Leeds, Ten Bells.

Langley (Tuesday/Thursday), and to Boxley (Friday). These routes all conveyed local passengers, thus competing with M & D buses as far as Hollingbourne Turn, Langley and Linton Corner and Corporation buses to Penenden Heath and the aged trams to Loose. Although Buck's were obliged to charge a penny over the tram fares (Maidstone Corporation was also the licensing authority and thus able to give some protection to its own services), they were clearly able to abstract traffic as the timetable included a Loose summary. It is interesting to note that by this time Coxheath, Boughton and Bearsted all had morning peak runs into town, although Leeds did not.

G.S. Wind's Red Road Cars began running in 1926, with an express service to London. In addition two local routes were operated, the Hollingbourne via Detling route mentioned in the introduction to this section and a daily Maidstone-Lenham via Ulcombe and Grafty Green. The former route had just two buses on weekdays, with two extras on Saturdays, as the two main villages had more frequent M & D services, and the thinly settled Pilgrim's Way between them yielded little traffic. The other service was more substantial with four through journeys, plus some short workings, including a weekday run from Grafty Green arriving at 08.48. A poor view was taken of Buck's (Cambrian's) intrusion on this route, as shown by a handwritten note added to the timetable in the M & D archive: 'A relief car is sent out at 1 o'clock to Pig & Whistle, then waits to return in front of the Cambrian coach.' Red Road Cars passed to M & D in April 1929.

Of the nineteen vehicles acquired from Weald of Kent in 1933 KJ77 lasted the longest; a 1931 AEC Regal, it was fitted with this 32-seat Harrington body in 1938 and survived until 1950. It is seen here working the Sevenoaks-Seal service. (M & D and East Kent Bus Club)

THORNS IN THE SIDE OF EAST SURREY

Mr C.M. Hever, a former East Surrey driver, started in business at Eynsford in 1927 and, from 15th March 1928, introduced a service to Dartford. The service ran via Horton Kirby and Darenth, with seven or eight trips a day under the fleetname Darenth Bus Services. East Surrey responded three days later over the same route with lower fares; Mr Hever responded by diverting via Farningham High Street and matching fares. Initially he seems to have got most of the traffic, quickly adding a second bus with the fleet later reaching four buses, all twenty-seat Beans. However he decided to sell the bus service to East Surrey from 26th July 1930, although he remained operating coaches until 1962. W.G. Hackney's Dartford & District Bus Service began operating on the same route in November 1930, but it ceased the following March after the Traffic Commissioners refused a licence.

Ted Newton's West Kent Motor Services Ltd commenced a Sevenoaks and Kemsing circular on 30th November 1927; it was the first service to that village, but it duplicated M & D's route 9 as far as Seal and East Surrey's 401 to Otford. M & D responded by introducing service 55 to Kemsing the following day, and East Surrey were able to exert enough pressure to get the service curtailed at Otford. East Surrey also had their second route (started December) to Westerham Hill diverted via Chipstead in lieu of Dunton Green. The firm survived the competition adding further routes in 1928 serving Heaverham and Godden Green, also Edenbridge/Brasted via Ide Hill and

Plaxtol via Ivy Hatch. A short lived route ran from Westerham to Tonbridge by way of Edenbridge and Penshurst. Their survival, however was not without cost. The operations of Penfold & Brodie of Green Street Green resulted in the Westerham Hill service being cut back to Knockholt, then completely withdrawn from May 1930. The Plaxtol route was turned back at Ivy Hatch within a year, and passed to M & D in February 1932, although the buses were sent to nearby Fawke Common instead. West Kent survived until 4th October 1939, when eight buses passed to London Transport and the Fawke Common and Kemsing via Seal routes were transferred to M & D.

Sevenoaks Motor Services started a route to Shoreham Village via Otford and the narrow lanes of Twitton with a fourteen-seat Chevrolet. It commenced on 24th November 1929, running hourly on Mondays to Fridays daytime – in the evenings and at weekends the bus was used for private hire, often going to the cinema at Tonbridge. Two Beans arrived in early 1930, allowing the service to be increased to half-hourly. East Surrey initially could only respond by running extras to Shoreham Station on route 401, as they were short of small buses at the time. With the acquisition of the Darenth Bus Services fleet, they were able to use some of those vehicles to introduce a service over the SMS route. As a result SMS sold out to East Surrey from 11th November 1930.

Autocar's KL9652, a 1925 AEC standing at Tunbridge Wells Opera House, with the office behind. This was one of the last buses with solid tyres.
(Pamlin Prints)

THE TUNBRIDGE WELLS BUS WAR

Finally in this section is this most famous and financially ruinous of all the local competition, the battle between Autocar and Redcar. Autocar, it will be recalled, had commenced in 1909 and had soon established itself as a soundly based firm. It attracted much local investment, enabling it to build a modern garage in Woodbury Park Road and to maintain a town centre office at the Opera House. By early 1914 the fleet had grown to fourteen Leyland saloons, with one of the original ABCs as a spare. The main route to Southborough ran every twenty minutes, with less frequent operation to Tonbridge (nine buses a day), Hadlow (6), Pembury (10), Rusthall (9), Speldhurst (6), Crowborough (5), Matfield (2), High Brooms (2), East Peckham (2), Hildenborough (4), Ticehurst (4) and Leigh and Penshurst (2). A bus also ran to Hawkenbury Cemetery on Wednesdays and several trips to the coast were operated. From 14th March 1914 a new thrice daily route to Maidstone was announced, but in fact it was no more than an extension to Mereworth to connect with M & D's new route from Maidstone. The war caused grave problems for Autocar who were reported as being left with only three modern Leylands and the original three ABCs, which had been stored for some time out of use. Routes were considerably thinned, with those to East Peckham, Hildenborough and Matfield being suspended.

Post-war expansion was rapid with operations being extended to Goudhurst, Hawkhurst, Farnborough, Edenbridge, Uckfield and Heathfield. There were some minor set backs, like Autocar's share of the Maidstone route being reduced to Hadlow and East Surrey's take over of the Farnborough route beyond Sevenoaks. Another route was shown to Gravesend, but certainly in latter days this was a connection with M & D at Borough Green.

In February 1924 a new firm, Redcar, appeared at Tunbridge Wells with a fleet of fast new small saloons. Redcar soon operated on most Autocar routes and even made minor extensions, for example to Cranbrook and Sandhurst; they ran in between the Autocar journeys, claiming that their intention was to give the public a better service and not to compete with Autocar. This did not impress Autocar who soon put chasers on Redcar timings. Other competition also appeared like Tunbridge Wells Victor, which ran a fleet of small Chevrolets from 1925 on various routes and Warren's Coaches of Ticehurst with a service from its home village, which was instigated in 1928. A little earlier Cooper of East Grinstead had begun a service to Tunbridge Wells via Forest Row in 1923; this ceased in June 1926 after some months of being shadowed by Autocar to Hartfield and East Surrey beyond — the following year these firms introduced a joint through service on this road. The rivalry between Autocar and Redcar came to a head in January 1928 when a fares war broke out; this got so bad that at one stage it was reported that empty deposit-paid bottles were accepted for fares; further spice was added when Redcar caused Autocar to be fined five shillings for operating a bus 0.3 inches wider than the legal maximum of seven foot six inches.

This quickly left both firms in a poor financial state. At first it seemed that a merger would take place, but this was forestalled by an early public announcement. Both East Surrey — who had already offered to buy Autocar in 1923 — and M & D took an interest in these events. East Surrey gained control of Autocar with the aid of

Autocar's Woodbury Park Road, Tunbridge Wells depot; KO3267 was Autocar 86, an ADC/Northern Counties of 1927.
(London Transport)

Representing the Redcar fleet is KO47 a 1927 Albion.
(M & D and East Kent Bus Club)

some LGOC capital, but before Redcar could be taken over a rescue agreement was reached with M & D.

Also, as a result of this, a working agreement was introduced from 1st May 1928; this stabilised the situation with a joint Redcar/ Autocar network with mileage and revenue pooled 45%/55%. The combined network featured routes to Sevenoaks, Cranbrook, Sandhurst, Burwash, Heathfield, Uckfield, Edenbridge via Penshurst or Cowden, Hadlow and Borough Green plus town services.

Following the takeover Autocar's mauve livery was changed to red and some standard LGOC buses soon appeared. Both East Surrey and Autocar became full LGOC subsidiaries in 1929.

An interesting mid-twenties view of Maidstone bus station; nearest the camera a 14-seat Guy/Beadle on 29 to Burham, then a pair of Tilling-Stevens on 1 to Gillingham and an ex-Neve Leyland (now rebodied by Beadle) on 12 to Headcorn.   (M & D and East Kent Bus Club)

KL1551 a Tilling-Stevens new in 1924 stands at the entrance of Gillingham depot.   (M & D and East Kent Bus Club)

M & D's expansion after the Great War was rapid, with large numbers of Leyland and Tilling-Stevens vehicles arriving and many new routes being started. Associated with this was the opening of several new premises to service the growing fleet. At Hastings a new 18-bus shed was opened at Brook Street in 1920, to replace a former banana warehouse in Earl Street. In the same year a small depot was also opened at Preston Street, Faversham; about this time a garage was opened in Winchester Road, Hawkhurst. At Gillingham the former shed at Fox Street was replaced in 1921 by a new garage in Nelson Road holding initially twenty-six buses; it was quickly increased to fifty-six and later to over a hundred buses and to include a bus station. 1922 saw two major infrastructure developments at Maidstone with the opening of the world's first bus station in Palace Avenue (just beating Derby) and the Central Works in Postley Road.

To help pay for this expansion Tilling capital arrived in 1921, along with Walter Wolsey as a director; the following year M & D became a public company with a capital of £200,000.

An early casualty was the system of allocating letters to routes, as it was soon realised that the alphabet would be exceeded. The

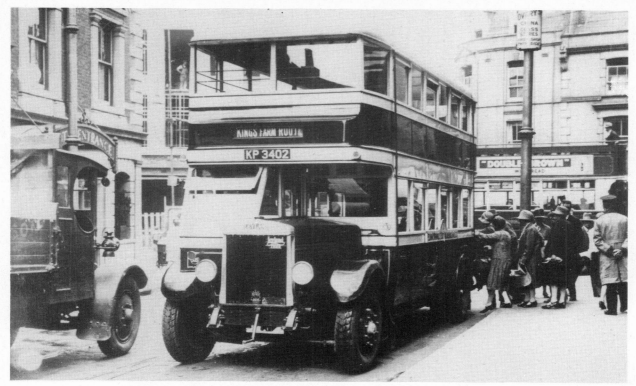

One of the Leyland bodied Leyland Titans that replaced the trams at Gravesend in 1929; it is on the Kings Farm route, known by the crews as the 'chicken run'.

more usual system of route numbers was adopted in 1920; the maximum extent of the letter system (with replacement numbers) was:

A	(1)	Maidstone-Chatham.
B	(2)	Chatham-Gravesend.
C	(3)	Maidstone-Sittingbourne-Faversham.
D	(4)	Chatham-Sittingbourne-Faversham.
E	(5)	Maidstone-Cranbrook-Hawkhurst.
F	(6)	Maidstone-Goudhurst.
G	(7)	Maidstone-Mereworth for Tunbridge Wells.
H	(8)	Maidstone-Hawkhurst-Hastings (later 5).
I	(9)	Maidstone-Malling-Sevenoaks.
J	(10)	Maidstone-Ashford.
K	(11)	Ashford-Faversham.
L	(12)	Maidstone-Tenterden.
M	(13)	Maidstone-Sutton Valence.
N	(14)	Tenterden-Ashford.
O	(15)	Hastings-Hailsham-Eastbourne.
P	(16)	Tenterden-Hastings.

Both O & P were post-war additions, with one bus being outstationed at Eastbourne from 28th June 1919 to work service O, which was later joined by a second bus to run route 26 to Pevensey. Development in Sussex was, however, limited by the growth of Southdown Motor Services Ltd of Brighton: an agreement was reached which resulted in Southdown taking over service 26 in May 1924 and the Eastbourne vehicle on what was now service 15 by the following year, although Southdown involvement began on this road by March 1921. 18 Hawkhurst-Brighton was introduced on 1st April 1920 and was possibly joint with Southdown from the outset. Another joint operation was 99 Eastbourne-Pevensey-Hastings, which was introduced on 29th March 1934, after the wider road was opened across Pevensey Marsh.

M & D's position in the Bexhill area was consolidated from 21st July 1926 with the acquisition of Carter & Lidstone Ltd of Little Common, who had been running local services since at least 1919.

In the north west of Kent the company's influence was extended in 1920 with the absorption of the North Kent bus fleet of the Gravesend & Northfleet Electric Tramways, and the next year a depot was opened at Gravesend Overcliffe. Two buses were outstationed at Borough Green from July 1922 to work services 22 to Gravesend and 25 Maidstone to Farningham, where another bus was based. A depot was built in Maidstone Road, Borough Green in 1926, resulting in the end of outstationing at Sevenoaks and Farningham. A twenty vehicle garage was opened at Priory Road, Dartford in May 1927.

The Gravesend & Northfleet trams were withdrawn on 28th February 1929, when the undertaking came into M & D control; sixteen Leyland Titans in red and cream were operated on replacement routes. The subsidiary was wound up on 31st December 1929 and the buses were then repainted into M & D livery. The new routes (in cases running beyond the tram lines) were 1 Denton-Gravesend-Swanscombe, 2 Gravesend-Kings Farm Estate circular via the Old Prince of Orange (the tram terminal) or Echo Square, 3 Gravesend Clock Tower-Northfleet Leather Bottel via Pelham Arms and 4 Clock Tower-Perry Street via Pelham Arms.

The next area for consolidation was the Medway Towns with the purchase of V. Vella's Theresie Safety Coaches of Chatham in January 1930; later that year the trams were replaced by buses (see Chatham and District section); 1931 saw the acquisition of Orange Coaches of Gillingham (operations included a Rainham-London service started in 1921) and the Medway District Bus Owners' Association, a consortium of many small operators — unfortunately little has so far come to light concerning early bus operations in this area.

Further acquisitions gave M & D control of the Tenterden area; the Weald of Kent Transport Co was taken over from 1st November 1933, with a fleet of nineteen buses, mainly Thornycrofts, and routes 1 Tenterden-Woodchurch-Ashford, 2/a/b Ashford-Pluckley-Tenterden/Egerton Forstal/Headcorn, 3 Rye-Hawkhurst, 7 Rye-London, and 8 Tenterden-London via Horsmonden; this was followed by the old established firm of R. & J. Bennett (The Times). They had been carriers for over a hundred years and had more recently run horse buses to Hastings and Maidstone (which ran until 1915 and was the last horse bus to serve Maidstone). Their final operation was the bus service between Tenterden and Rye, which passed to M & D in 1935. This firm's relationship with M & D had always been good and at one stage Bennett's yard was used by M & D's buses.

Unlike in many areas the railways played little part in the development of bus services in Kent — they did run a few horse buses like Ashford to New Romney and a single short-lived venture into motor bus operation.

However the Southern Railway (Road Transport) Act, 1928 gave the Southern Railway powers to take part in the provision of bus services, and this was reflected in the purchase of shares in both M & D and East Kent. This resulted in an era of road/rail co-operation, with interavailability of tickets and improvements to interchange facilities. Notable developments included the provision of railway land for Sheerness Bus Station (1930) and Rye depot in 1939, although Rye was requisitioned for military use on completion.

Three East Kent buses foregather at Deal, South Parade about 1920. Former Margate, Canterbury and District Daimlers (with newer char-a-banc bodies) KT384/7228 were working to Dover and Margate respectively, while a Tilling-Stevens saloon for Canterbury waits behind.

EAST KENT
ROAD CAR COMPANY LTD

In a ditch on its way to Ramsgate is FN8313, a Daimler rebuilt by East Kent and fitted with a 36-seat Short Bros body in 1927.

(M & D and East Kent Bus Club)

The only Isle of Thanet Tramway buses to last any time with East Kent were five Daimler COG5s; one of these, CKP878, still in original livery but showing an East Kent service number, is seen at Ramsgate Harbour in 1937,

(M & D and East Kent Bus Club)

East Kent's growth in the twenties and thirties followed a similar path to that of M & D; fleet strength was rapidly increased by Tilling-Stevens and Daimler vehicles, often bodied or rebodied in the company's own bodyshop. It is notable that no double-deckers were operated (barring two purchased from Sayer of Margate in 1919, that were run for only three months) until 1927, when three second-hand bodies from LGOC were mounted on some of the last of the reconditioned Daimler chassis to enter service. As a result the following year a batch of Leyland Tigers with Short Bros of Rochester open-top double-deckers arrived; the first of the closed-top Leyland Titans were delivered in 1930. After a brief flirtation with Morris Commercial buses, including the rare Viceroy double-decker, Leyland and Dennis became the usual choice of manufacturer by the mid-thirties.

At Canterbury a new garage was built at St Stephens in 1925, permitting the original depot in Kirby Lane to be developed fully as the Central Works. In Dover the Russell Street site was first occupied in 1923 and the garage at Station Road, Ashford was opened in 1926. Several small premises were owned in the Thanet area, including at Dane Road, Margate, which was in use as a coachworks by 1922 and later used for winter storage; the present location at Margate Road, Westwood was acquired in 1927. This and many of the other depots have subsequently been rebuilt and extended and several small depots and outstations have been operated from time to time; in 1932 a new depot was opened at Rye, South Undercliffe replacing a former shed on the same site used since the early 1920s.

The railway interest was revealed by the building of Seabrook garage in 1931 on the site of the former Sandgate station, and the replacement of the Canterbury to Whitstable line in December 1930 by East Kent buses. Several small firms in the Whitstable district were purchased in the late twenties: Fitt of Tankerton (1925), Cook (Royal Native) of Whitstable and Wood of Blean (both 1926) and Klein & Stanton (Whitstable Town Bus Service) in 1929. A small garage was acquired from Wood Bros in the Horsebridge in 1927 and was used by the bus working the service to Canterbury via Tyler Hill.

East Kent did not use a route numbering system until 1937 (although there is evidence of a very short-lived system in c.1917), when it introduced a very logical system that lasted basically unaltered until 1971. It started with the rural routes from Canterbury numbered clockwise 1 to Ashford, 2 to Hastings, 3 to Faversham, 4 to Whitstable etc, then the Canterbury City services (23-29). It then continued round the coast from Faversham to Rye then Ashford and finally Hastings. Joint routes 10 & 67 retained their M & D numbers and some spares were left for future growth.

Some major acquisitions not covered already were Sims (Earlswood Bus Co Ltd) of Westgate with three buses and the 36-coach Redbourne Group of Ramsgate (running since 1913) both in 1935. On 1st January 1937 East Kent buses replaced the Dover trams running Marine Station (now Western Docks) to River and Buckland and Monument to Maxton. Control of the Isle of Thanet services came finally in October 1936, but no major physical changes took place until 25th March 1937, when the trams were replaced by East Kent buses.

CONTROL AND LEGISLATION

The first attempt to control the chaotic bus industry came in London in 1924. Before then, anyone with a bus approved by the Inspector of Carriages of the Metropolitan Police, and who paid the necessary hackney carriage fee, could put a bus onto the road. In the post-war years expansion was rapid, with many new firms appearing, usually directly competing with established bus or tram operators on the busy trunk routes. Financial failures were frequent and the competition cut-throat.

The London Traffic Act of 1924 gave the Police control of routes, terminal points and the number of buses/operators on each route. Incidentally, the Police devised a service number system which still provides the basis of the London Transport and London Country system today. Called the Bassom System after the policeman in charge of this department at the time, it gave each service a unique number regardless of operator, with short workings denoted by a suffix letter, although this particular aspect evolved to cover variations of route. In Central London many numbers already used by the LGOC group were unchanged, but East Surrey's services were re-numbered into the system from December 1924.

Although the 1924 Act reduced competition on the routes, many new services were allowed; these routes provided some useful fresh links in the suburbs, but as a rule they generally duplicated some existing facilities, especially in the central area.

THE ROAD TRAFFIC ACT

The 1930 Road Traffic Act introduced a nationwide control of the industry similar to that of the 1924 London Act, but under the control of the newly formed Traffic Commissioners.

The new legislation required that a Road Service Licence was obtained from the Traffic Commissioners for all stage and express services and tours and excursions, leaving only private hire outside the scope of the Act. The RSL covered fares, route and timetable and to make even the smallest change needed an alteration to the RSL. From the early stages it was made clear that not all existing operations would be granted RSLs, particularly where competition was intense. For some operators this was too much and many sold out or concentrated on private hire, but equally others went the opposite way, prompting this ministerial warning: 'The Minister of Transport has deemed it desirable to sound a note of warning concerning the recent establishment of a number of new motor-coach and bus services. Many of them are believed to be superfluous to the requirement of the travelling public and, in official circles, it is thought that the operators have hurriedly entered this field of enterprise or have suddenly decided to extend their activities before Part IV of the RTA comes into operation (this was after 8th February 1931, the last day of uncontrolled entry into new services), in order to establish a claim to consideration when the new system of licensing and control of public-service vehicles takes effect.' No doubt this criticism included the new Green Line routes that appeared in Kent at this time, to Westerham via Bromley (October 1930), Edenbridge via Croydon (December 1930), Dartford and Farningham (both January 1931). The notice continues: 'Some local authorities, mindful of their languishing powers, may have become lax in the exercise of their function as licensing bodies and have issued indiscriminately licences to ply for hire. Such a policy must inevitably, at a later date, create confusion.'

And indeed confusion there was as the Traffic Commissioners sat to consider the various applications and counter applications. The chairman of the South Eastern Traffic Commissioners was Mr Rowland Harker who was soon to gain a reputation as an ardent supporter of cross-subsidisation, by giving priority on profitable routes to firms who also worked thinner routes. The MT Company of New Cross were very incensed by this policy as East Kent were granted licences for a number of Thanet-London services, despite the fact that MT had pioneered the service. Neither did it help Mr E. Mears who was refused a licence for his Sittingbourne-London route and the Sittingbourne local, both of which had run for over two years. Goodsell of Shottenden even failed to apply for a licence until 1935; not surprisingly this was refused and East Kent asked to take over.

Although the system caused much anguish during its introduction, it stood the test of time, giving a firm base to the industry for nearly fifty years. For the larger companies the new system had the advantage of centralising licensing. East Kent, for example, had previously dealt with no less than twenty-two different Local Authorities, often imposing their own local conditions. The Act also increased the maximum speed for buses to 30 mph, and introduced the first control of drivers' hours.

Below: Some local bus tickets through the years.

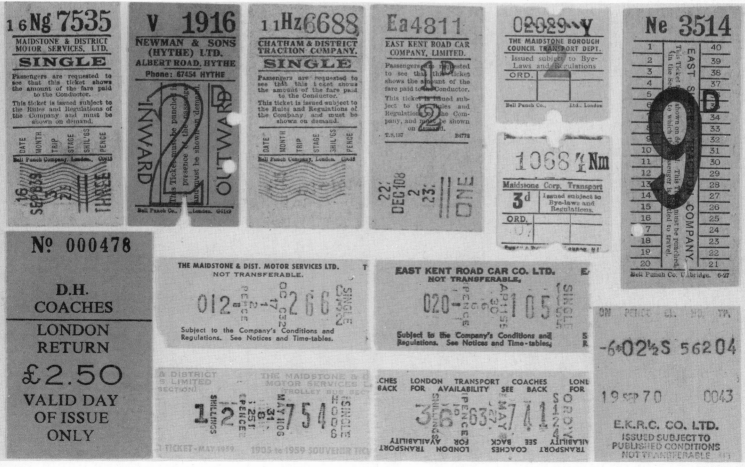

A Timpson's Karrier at Lamberhurst, probably on the London and Hastings express service.

East Kent buses at Herne Bay rescue stranded railway passengers in September 1919.
(M & D and East Kent Bus Club)

Auto Pilots of Folkestone ran this Dennis Lancet, with unusual 31-seat Duple observation bodywork; it passed to East Kent in 1935, who ran it for two years. (M & D and East Kent Bus Club)

DY5722, a Timpson AEC Reliance at Boundary Road, Ramsgate on the London service in the early thirties.

LONG DISTANCE COACH SERVICES

It was not until after World War I that regular long distance coach services were again considered after the Handcross Hill accident. In September 1919 a sudden railway strike left many holidaymakers stranded all round the Kent coast; this prompted both East Kent and M & D to run special journeys to London, pressing into service every available vehicle. East Kent introduced a Thanet-Maidstone-London service in May 1921, a year after MT Company (Motor Coaches) Ltd of New Cross had pioneered the route. An early cross country route was East Kent's Margate-Folkestone-Hastings introduced on 12th July 1920. M & D's first express services from Maidstone and Gillingham to London were introduced in 1923.

Another pioneer was Alexander Timpson of Plumstead, who ran horse brakes from 1896; prior to the war he operated three char-a-bancs. The chassis were requisitioned but the bodies were stored till 1919, when they were fitted to new Karrier chassis and used on a service to Hastings. In 1920 a former tram depot at Catford was purchased and services were offered to various resorts including Thanet. Further developments included an extensive network of feeder services from all over east London; in 1923 the London-Hastings service was running thrice daily and in 1926 a Herne Bay run was added; Sheerness was served for the 1931 season only, before M & D took over.

Timpson's did have two brief flirtations with stage operation, at Hastings and on route 289 Plumstead Common-Blackheath-Bromley Common (-Westerham Hill on Sundays); this began in March 1923 and passed to LGOC control in 1928. In 1926 the firm became A. Timpson & Son Ltd, and passed to BET in 1944. The firm remained a major coach operator running to many South Coast resorts from the head office at Catford, and depots at Crayford and Croydon; a small shed at Boundary Road, Ramsgate was maintained until 1968. This firm now forms part of National London, although many of the express services are worked by Green Line.

Two other early express coach operators were London Coastal Coaches and Samuelson Transport; both began running these services in 1920, and indeed by the end of the season Samuelsons were running over a hundred coaches, serving resorts from Yarmouth to Portsmouth. London Coastal Coaches also ran a central booking point in Lower Belgrave Street, Victoria which was used by many operators, including East Kent and M & D, although some of the former's coaches continued to use Shoolbred's store in Tottenham Court Road. In April 1928 they moved to a larger site at Lupus Street, Pimlico, and returned to Victoria on 10th March 1932 with the opening of the new custom built coach station in Buckingham Palace Road, which is still the focal point for express services from all over the country. It is many years since LCC have actually operated any coaches, although Samuelson ran a small fleet of private hire coaches until absorbed by National Travel South East (now National London) in 1974; their depot adjacent to Victoria Coach Station is still used to fuel and service coaches using Victoria.

Athol Murray Kemp-Gee's Cambrian Coaching of Brixton began a London-Folkestone route in 1921, quickly adding other routes including the Brighton-Ashford-Margate service, which had been pioneered by Vanguard of Brighton also in 1921. Cambrian ran buses in London from 1923 to 1926, and sold out its Kent operations in November 1929.

Many other firms followed and it was in this area that many disputes arose with the introduction of route licensing in 1931. MT Company's disquiet at the refusal of some of its workings in favour of East Kent has already been mentioned; another dispute arose over the London-Dover service of Express Safety Coaches of London. This route ran via Maidstone but the Traffic Commissioners suggested it should run via Rochester, a move that quickly brought an objection from Rochester City Council on the grounds of traffic congestion. This service passed to East Kent on 21st December 1934 and around this time it acquired all the remaining daily services to this part of the coast. These were: Russell Motor Service, Hawkinge running Folkestone-London (1930), Pullman Saloon of Broadstairs, Ramsgate to London service (1933), Orange Luxury Coaches of London's routes to Dover and Deal (April 1935), Orange Motor Co (Dover) Ltd also running London to Dover (June 1935), Auto Pilots Ltd, Folkestone again working from its home town to the capital (December 1935) and finally in May 1937 the remaining licences of MT Company of New Cross from the Thanet area.

On 25th March 1929 Elliot Bros (Royal Blue) began a coach service from its home town of Bournemouth to Margate, running right along the South Coast. To compete with this a joint East Kent/Southdown/Wilts & Dorset service over the same route was started two months later. Subsequently Royal Blue became part of the BET/Tilling empire and they replaced Wilts & Dorset on the joint service, which became known as the South Coast Express.

August 1930 saw M & D introduce an extensive network of limited stop services using a fleet of new Leyland Tigers. These included daily runs from Gillingham to Portsmouth and Eastbourne and from Dartford to Margate; another service from Dartford gave day facilities alternately to Eastbourne and Brighton. These routes were later expanded into the West Country, jointly operated with Royal Blue and the Cheltenham-centred Associated Motorways pool.

In 1934 M & D acquired the Stratford-Chatham service of Fleet Transport Services of Stratford that they had begun in 1930, giving them a footing in East London, that was subsequently developed into a Leyton to Sheppey service. Even so the majority of services to the Kent coast from this area remained in the independent sector, with firms like Grey Green, Lacey of East Ham and Harris of Grays still providing summer weekend express services.

It was not only London to the coast traffic that attracted new coach services during the twenties and thirties, but also limited stop services from the country towns around London; many of these routes were the forerunners of the Green Line network.

Glenton of New Cross ran a London-Sevenoaks service for a while during 1927, and Safeway Motor Services tried a similar operation in 1929/30. Redcar began its frequent Tunbridge Wells-London via Tonbridge, Sevenoaks and Bromley service on 16th September 1927 although operation through the following winter was somewhat erratic. it soon became established and was joined by Warren's Coaches running a couple of journeys over a similar route, but starting back from their home village of Ticehurst. In pre-RTA days these routes

Lined-up outside the head office are some of M & D's Leyland Tiger/Harrington coaches that pioneered many of their limited-stop services.

(M & D and East Kent Bus Club)

Standing in the Autocar bus station at Tunbridge Wells is a Green Line AEC Regal on the London service. (London Transport)

could also carry short-distance passengers, and soon the LGOC group became concerned at the loss of revenue to this type of service. As a result they began to run their own coach routes, with Autocar starting an hourly London service on 6th June 1930. On 9th July 1930 a new subsidiary, Green Line, was formed to run such services.

Blue Belle Motors Ltd, SW9 began a London-Godstone-Westerham service on 1st October 1930 and Green Line countered a week later with a similar service (worked by East Surrey vehicles from Dunton Green), that was quickly extended to Sevenoaks. Blue Belle replied with a service via Bromley, but sold out to Green Line on 20th July 1932.

Other Green Line routes followed rapidly and by February 1931, when a letter code system was introduced, Kent routes were A Dartford, I Farningham, J Edenbridge, L Sevenoaks/Tunbridge Wells.

Green Line opened their own coach station on 8th January 1931 at Poland Street, off Oxford Street. As mentioned on page 25, many routes were introduced just before the introduction of the RTA and initially the Metropolitan Traffic Commissioners refused licences for about a third of the Green Line network; further difficulties arose from a proposed ban on coaches in central London, to ease congestion around Oxford Circus. All this resulted in considerable public outcry and a committee of enquiry; no change was in fact made until London Transport days when the Green Line routes were recast in October 1933.

Poland Street was closed and the majority of routes diverted to Victoria, many running on a cross-London basis; a 25% loss of traffic resulted in the removal from the central area, although the rest of the network was secured.

To close this section here is another quote from the Red Road Cars of Maidstone's timetable: 'Red Road Cars ran their first journey on Monday 15th November 1926, to London — the only service to the heart of the West End (Oxford Circus), and were pioneers of the Theatre Car which leaves London at 11.30 on Wednesday and Saturday nights. From the early spring of 1927 a service of three journeys a day has been maintained, with an extra journey on Wednesdays and Saturdays, the return fare being 5/- until December 1st 1927, when, owing to the reduction of railway fares, the day return was reduced to 4/-. At the same time, in order to encourage more people to travel on Wednesday afternoons, a special excursion coach was run at 3/6 return, which has proved very popular.'

Northfleet Depot soon after takeover by London Transport, with a former M & D Leyland Titan still in its old colours on the left.   (London Transport)

THE FORMATION OF LONDON TRANSPORT

Further legislation for London was still under consideration by a Royal Commission and, following the Traffic Commissioners' rejection of a third of the Green Line network, a Committee of Enquiry was held into this aspect. The Green Line services emerged virtually unscathed, except for the banning of coaches in the heart of London, which moved the focus of the Green Line network from Oxford Circus to Victoria, where it remains today.

The Royal Commission recommended the formation of a new public body to control buses, trolleybuses, and trams in Greater London, together with the Underground Railways. The designated area for this new body was roughly sixty-five miles north-south and fifty miles east-west; the body was also empowered to operate services ten miles beyond this monopoly area, subject to obtaining the necessary licence from the Traffic Commissioners – a requirement that did not apply in the monopoly area. In Kent this outer zone was reduced to five miles, following pressure at the Parliamentary Committee stage.

Thus the London Passenger Act, 1933, was passed with the new body, the London Passenger Transport Board, taking over its duties on 1st July 1933.

The bus department was based on the LGOC operating practice and several features were inherited from it, including the fleet numbering system, the use of depot codes, running numbers, and of course the famous red livery. LGOC contributed 4,039 buses, with the next largest, Tilling, a mere 364 vehicles.

Despite a number of recent takeovers by LGOC just prior to 1933, more than fifty bus operators' services were absorbed by the Central (red) area of LPTB. In the Country (green) area many operations were also taken over. Another complication was that the new LPTB area did not coincide with the various territorial agreements the LGOC group had made with adjoining operators. This meant that LPTB had to purchase part of the operation of firms like Eastern National, Aldershot & District and of course M & D. Furthermore in Kent the operations of Autocar, the LGOC subsidiary, extended well beyond the LPTB area. The main results of the 1933 Act in Kent were as follows: M & D's Dartford and Northfleet depots passed to London Transport, together with the former tram routes at Gravesend and 27 Gravesend to Ash. Other M & D routes were curtailed at the boundary; 25 Maidstone-Farningham, at Wrotham, 26 Dartford-Faversham, and 57 Dartford-Strood-Maidstone, both at Gravesend, and 42 Dartford-Longfield-Gillingham, at Meopham.

At the same time M & D's London coaches ceased to convey local passengers within the LPTB area, ceasing to call at Dartford completely. London Transport replacements included the extension of the Green Line routes to Farningham and Dartford to Wrotham and Gravesend respectively. New routes were 485 Wrotham-Farningham, 486 Dartford-Gravesend-Denton, the old tram terminus – for many years M & D could not carry local passengers between Denton and the centre of Gravesend, even on local routes serving the new estates

in the east of the town, which was M & D territory, 487/8/92-7 Gravesend locals, 489/90 Gravesend-Ash and 491 Dartford-Meopham (Hook Green). A token presence was kept by M & D at Dartford with the continued operation of a number of limited stop runs to coastal resorts during the summer. In return M & D gained control of most of the Autocar operations at Tunbridge Wells, including the larger of the two depots (St Johns Road) and the Opera House office. LPTB retained the Green Line service to London, the Tonbridge-Sevenoaks stage service (as 402a) and beyond East Grinstead on the Tunbridge Wells to Reigate run. To work the Green Line service the small depot at Whitefield Road and the Lime Hill Road coach station in Tunbridge Wells were also kept by LPTB. Also it acquired the Bexley and Erith UDCs' tram network, which was converted to trolley bus operation in November 1935.

On the vehicle side 55 M & D buses passed to London Transport, mainly Leyland Titan double-deckers and Leyland Tiger coaches. One strange feature was that London Transport were not keen to accept lowbridge buses (that is with a sunken side gangway upstairs), so most of the lowbridge examples at Dartford and Northfleet were kept by M & D and highbridge ones from other depots were sent to LPTB.

Over a brief period of several months London Transport also absorbed a number of smaller operators within its area. Those germane to this book are listed below:

Gravesend & District Bus Services Ltd of Pelham Road South was the largest of these with eight buses; this firm was registered in 1924 and ran routes to Dartford, Northfleet and locals to Gloster Road, Park Avenue and Poplar Avenue which passed to LPTB on 1st October 1933. An earlier run to Wrotham had ceased in 1931.

Greenhithe & District Bus Service of H.M. Howells had three buses working a route from Dartford to Gravesend via Bean; this passed to LPTB in April 1934.

The one bus operation of R.E. Hollands, Longfield working from Dartford to Ash was absorbed in January 1934.

Further south the only stage service not already taken over by East Surrey was Penfold & Brodie of Green Street Green. Although the routes from Westerham Hill to Sevenoaks and Green Street Green to Knockholt passed to LPTB, this firm remained in the coach business for many years.

The Autocar fleet remained an M & D subsidiary, as it was not possible to amend the pool working arrangements with Redcar, despite a small amount of M & D involvement in the latter firm. In 1935, however, Redcar finally agreed to sell out to M & D, the actual date being on 1st January, although it was some weeks before physical changes took place. This allowed the ending of the 1928 pooling agreement and the Autocar subsidiary was wound up from 1st May 1935; some buses gained M & D colours prior to this date. Services in the Tunbridge Wells area were recast and numbered into the M & D series; for the first time buses ran through between Maidstone and

TD152 (KP3393) was one of only two of the Gravesend tram replacement buses to pass to London Transport; this was the third livery carried by this bus.   (London Transport)

DGY403, a typical London Transport trolleybus leaving the Dartford terminus on the 696 route to Woolwich.   (Pamlin Prints)

Reflecting the M & D era of Autocar is KO119, a 1927 Tilling-Stevens that was transferred to Autocar in 1934 after fitting a new Eastern Counties body.
(M & D and East Kent Bus Club)

Backbone of the post war London Transport fleet was the famous AEC 'RT' type; RT2729 leaves the Dartford Tunnel on the short-lived service from Grays.
(London Transport)

Tunbridge Wells, as the respective services were linked at Hadlow and East Peckham. The position was further consolidated by M & D also acquiring Tunbridge Wells Victor on 9th May 1935.

Redcar's Tonbridge-Sevenoaks and Tunbridge Wells-London routes passed to London Transport from 31st July 1935.

The Autocar fleet of eighty-two vehicles that passed to M & D control was mainly AEC, a make not associated with M & D at this time. Before the Autocar fleet was merged with the parent fleet some newly rebodied Tilling-Stevens were transferred in; the first sign of M & D influence.

The Redcar fleet added another fifty-four vehicles, of which nine were transferred to London Transport.

As mentioned in the introduction, it is not proposed to consider in great detail London Transport's role in Kent as many records of this already exist. The many motley acquired buses were fairly quickly replaced by standard vehicles, mostly AECs.

The former tram depot at Northfleet was replaced by a new building in London Road in 1937; its architecture is typical of the many capital projects undertaken in this era by London Transport.

The post war resumption of the Green Line routes saw the introduction of the 7xx number series in place of the previous letter system; those serving Kent were: 701 Gravesend-Ascot, 702 Gravesend-Sunningdale, 703 Wrotham-Amersham, 704 Tunbridge Wells-Windsor, 705 Sevenoaks-Windsor, 706 Westerham-Aylesbury. The first of the famous RF coaches appeared on 704 in 1951, and the first orbital route 725 Gravesend-Dartford-Bromley-Croydon-Kingston-Windsor proved successful when introduced in 1953.

The RF was also used on the rural bus routes, with the RT double-decker working the busier routes; these were joined in the mid-sixties by the first of the coach and country bus Routemasters. These were used on 705/6, with the bus version running on many of the urban routes from Northfleet.

Recalling an earlier period is LH8694, a Gravesend & District Daimler in Dartford on the trunk route to Gravesend in 1914. (Pamlin Prints)

In 1963 the opening of the Dartford Tunnel allowed some new routes to be introduced, but London Transport's operation of these proved short-lived; a fleet of Ford Thames buses with cycle racks in place of the lower deck were also operated on behalf of the Tunnel Board, but with only a negligible demand from cyclists to use the tunnel Land Rovers soon proved to be adequate.

In 1962 the Bexleyheath based trolleybuses were replaced by motor buses; replacement service 96 Woolwich-Dartford is the only London Transport route to serve Dartford since the formation of London Country in 1970.

Chatham & District 363 (KR8141) was one of the tram replacement Leyland Titans; note the enclosed stairs. (Pamlin Prints)

GKE79, one of the pre-war Weymann bodied Bristol K types in Globe Lane, Chatham. (M & D and East Kent Bus Club)

The Chatham & District Traction Company was a statutory undertaking which lasted just twenty-five years from the replacement of the trams on 1st October 1930.

The Chatham & District Light Railways began running trams in June 1902 and by 1908 had completed an extensive network, reaching as far as Strood Hill and Rainham. One unusual feature was that all the lines in the Borough of Rochester were built by the Corporation but operated by the C&DLR under a working agreement.

The Chatham & District Traction Act, 1929, made provision for the trams to be replaced by buses; this took effect from 1st October 1930, when a fleet of thirty-three new Leyland Titans in light green, brown and cream entered service from the former tram depot at Luton. It was a subsidiary of M & D, with its legal address at Maidstone (M & D bought an interest in the tramway in 1927), and statutory powers to operate services within twelve miles of Chatham Town Hall, although in practice they only operated the former tram routes and their subsequent extensions.

Initial routes were:
1 Luton-Chatham-Dockyard
2 Chatham Cemetery-Chatham-Jezreels-Rainham Webster Road
3 Frindsbury-Rochester-Chatham-Brompton-Gillingham-Gillingham Green
4 Strood Hill-Rochester-Chatham
5 Borstal-Rochester-Chatham-Jezreels-Gillingham-Strand.

These were gradually extended into new housing areas; in 1933 route 2 to Huntsmans Corner, route 4 to Strood, Rede Court and in Frindsbury some buses were diverted from the original Bingham Road terminus to turn at Slatin Road as 3a; in 1937 route 1 to Wagon-at-Hale on Friday evenings and Saturdays (this was mainly for people going there for country walks and was withdrawn in 1940 as an economy measure), route 2 reached Magpie Hall Road and route 3a Brompton Farm Road; and in 1942 every third journey on route 5 was diverted at Upper Delce to Cookham Wood as 5a.

Post war expansion was mainly in the Wayfield area; in 1945 alternate route 1s were extended to Wagon-at-Hale and Churchill Avenue, followed in 1950 by Mountbatten Avenue and finally in 1952 on to Burma Way. This service was strengthened by extending route 4 alternately to Wagon-at-Hale (replacing route 1 — all journeys now going up Wayfield Road) and Churchill Avenue; the next year the 4 was further extended so both routes ran to Burma Way. One final addition to the route mileage came in 1955, when route 2 was sent up Walderslade Road — almost passing the Burma Way terminus — to the Weeds Wood Estate.

Former Chatham Guy Arab TKM356 was still at work in Chatham after becoming M & D DH462 in 1955. (M & D and East Kent Bus Club)

On the vehicle front ten more Titans entered service in 1931, replacing some open-top Tilling-Stevens loaned by M & D. Indeed on paper all the initial forty-three Titans were owned by M & D and hired to C & D; they passed into full C & D ownership by 1934.

In 1937 a start was made on modernising the fleet when four Bristol GO5Gs entered traffic; these were found to be unsuitable for local work and the chassis were sent back to Bristol (subsequently entering service as tram replacements at Bath), and the bodies were fitted to four Bristol K5Gs in 1938. These were found to be satisfactory and another thirty-seven arrived in 1939 along with three Titans. Some utility Bristol K5Gs were allocated to C & D in 1942, which allowed the remaining Leylands to be transferred to the M & D fleet. Three Guy Arabs came in 1944, but were swapped in 1946 with Bristol K5Gs from M & D to maintain standardisation on Bristols at Luton; such inter-fleet exchanges or loans were a regular feature over the years.

For the third generation of C & D buses Guy Arabs were chosen; batches of eight being delivered in both 1953 and 1954. A third batch due in 1955 was delivered direct to M & D, as the C & D operation was wound up after service on 30th September. The decision to end C & D was made by the parent company in order to integrate all the services in the Medway Towns, but as it was a statutory company parliamentary powers were necessary. These were granted, despite opposition led by Gillingham Council in favour of municipal control, under the Chatham & District Traction Act, 1955. Before entering service on 1st October all the buses had M & D fleetnames applied and they were quickly repainted into M & D green and cream. Bus 919 (GKR 743) was the last C & D vehicle to operate and also the first to run with an M & D scroll, by virtue of working on the early and late staff bus duties.

Crossing Maidstone Bridge is one of the original Ransomes trolleybuses, with a Tilling-Stevens bus behind.   (Irene Hales Collection)

MAIDSTONE CORPORATION TRANSPORT

Maidstone is today served by the only remaining example of a municipal public transport service in the area; the first Corporation service was the Barming tram route in 1904, followed by lines to Loose (1907) and Tovil (1908). Prior to the opening of the tram routes there was a horse bus service from Barming Asylum to the cemetery; another route was from London Road to the North Ward area, and was subject to brief motor bus operation by the Commercial Motor Co from July 1908. After various discussions by the Corporation on how to serve this area, it was decided that motor buses would be cheaper than trams. Accordingly the necessary powers were obtained in the Maidstone Corporation Act, 1923, and the first route, Penenden Heath-London Road, began on 7th April 1924 worked by locally built Tilling-Stevens petrol-electric saloons; this was followed by Park Avenue-Hackney Road from 14th May 1926.

The original tram equipment was by this time wearing out and on 1st May 1928 the Barming route was converted to trolleybus operation; powers for this were in the 1923 Act, plus an enabling Order of 1927. The lightly used Tovil line was replaced by motor buses from 1st August 1929 and from 12th February 1930 the Loose service was operated by trolleys, together with a new bifurcation at the Wheatsheaf to Grove Road. Since 1928 this had been partially covered by a bus service to Mangravet Avenue, and this was now switched to Foster Clark Estate. Further new routes followed rapidly: Queens Road (1930), Tillings Works (1932), Mote Park Estate (1934), Plains Avenue (1938). The first double-deck motor buses arrived in 1934, and no more saloons were purchased until 1975. Post-war routes included Ringlestone (1946), Palace Wood (1959), Banky Meadow (1965), Gatland Lane (1968), Senacre Wood (1970) and Vinters Park (1971). Other services were extended as housing spread around the town. On the London Road, Allington Way was reached in 1950, and in Shepway stages of growth were Kent Road (1948), Derby Road (1952), Oxford Road (also 1952), and Westmorland Road (1956). Along the Sutton Road trolleybuses were extended to Nottingham Avenue (1954), Brishing Lane (1959), and Park Wood Shops (1963); at the Barming end the Bull Inn was reached in 1947. The original trolleybus fleet was replaced by 1947 and subsequent needs were covered by second-hand purchases from Llanelli, Hastings and Brighton as their systems closed. The end of the Maidstone trolleybus came on 15th April 1967, in the face of rising costs and inflexibility of operation.

The livery had always been brown (of various shades) with white or cream, but in 1965 a bright new colour scheme of light blue and cream was introduced on the first batch of eight Leyland Atlanteans (rear engined, front-entrance, double-deckers) purchased for trolleybus replacement. The previous generation of twenty-six Leyland Titans and one of three early post-war Daimlers retained beyond their time to aid trolleybus replacement were also repainted in this livery. The Atlanteans were used to introduce one-man-operation,

At the Barming, Bull Inn turning circle in 1966 is HKR7, a 1946 Sunbeam with a Northern Coachbuilders body, with GKP512, a wartime example that was rebodied by Roe in 1960.   (R.I. Stacey)

A surprise purchase in 1976 was fourteen 'Lilac Leopards' from Nottingham; HNU123N was working service 88 (London Road to Hatherall Road) in this 1979 view.

initially just Sundays and evenings, but soon even the former trolley bus roads were fully OMO. In 1969 a new depot was opened at Armstrong Road, replacing the former tram depot in Tonbridge Road.

From 1st April 1974, as part of a national local government reorganisation, it became The Maidstone Borough Council, with an enlarged area covering the rural communities south and west of the town. At the same time a new Transport Officer was appointed and a number of policy changes soon became evident. On the vehicle front single deckers replaced all of the double-deckers by early 1979.

Ironically the Atlanteans went early because of their high resale value (the 1972 batch served only five years), leaving Titan 26 the last example in use on peak trips until March 1979; it is now preserved. In 1976 the new Bedford saloons were supplemented by fourteen Leyland Leopard coaches purchased from Nottingham, which entered service in their lilac/maroon livery. Since then second-hand vehicles and manufacturers' demonstrators have been a regular feature of the fleet, the latter often being purchased after a period of loan. Most notable was the use of all four Bedford JJL rear-engined minibuses built, three of which were bought. In 1979 one Bedford was painted in the brown and cream tram livery to celebrate seventy-five years of operation. This was subsequently adopted as standard for buses, with coaches in dark blue and cream; with the second-hand vehicles there have been times when as many as ten different colour schemes could be seen, in a fleet of just under fifty. On the operations side private hire has been developed as a useful source of revenue and a number of school contracts obtained.

A 'Park and Ride' service introduced in 1975 did not last long, nor did a Staplehurst minibus service tried the following year. Many services were diverted via the new Stoneborough Centre from 15th November 1976 and extensive town centre rerouting took place from 12th November 1978 with the opening of St Peter's Bridge, and at the same time service numbers were introduced for the first time ever.

The new Maidstone Hospital at Barming gave rise to further service revisions from 29th July 1983, when several routes were extended to serve it and link it with Barming Station. CKM138Y, one of the Wright bodied Bedfords, stops at the Hospital on its way to the railway station.

The remains of three M & D Leyland Titans after the raid on Gillingham Depot on 27th August 1940.
(M & D and East Kent Bus Club)

A wartime view of Canterbury Bus Station, with one bus in the red and grey camouflage livery; in the distance a M & D utility Daimler arrives on the service from Maidstone.
(M & D and East Kent Bus Club)

WORLD WAR TWO

World War II had a drastic effect on the bus industry of this country and Kent, in its front line position, had more than its fair share of trouble.

The first effect, just prior to the declaration of war, was the withdrawal of the entire Green Line network on 31st August 1939, as all the coaches had been modified so that they could easily be adapted as ambulances. Initially not all were needed in this role and there was a limited reintroduction of services to Gravesend and Tunbridge Wells in early 1940; further improvements were made in December 1940, when a temporary numbering system was introduced and service 2 Gravesend-London gained double-deck operation. These continued until 29th September 1942, when the growing shortage of fuel and tyres resulted in the Government's instruction to withdraw the services.

The industry had to cope with vastly changed traffic patterns. With the evacuation of much of the civilian population and the loss of the Kent coast holiday traffic East Kent had surplus buses. Timetables were often cut, but additional work was gained in troop movements or transporting factory and dockyard workers, as the war effort increased. Drivers and vehicles were liable to be requisitioned by the military at short notice; for the Dunkirk evacuation in June 1940 East Kent supplied about 250 buses to move troops to London. Many vehicles, especially coaches, were permanently requisitioned by the War Department: East Kent alone lost 118 vehicles in this way during 1940.

The blackout was an early difficulty for the bus operator. Although some evening services were cut, it was still necessary to run buses during the blackout — especially in the winter months. Headlights were masked or replaced by smaller lights of limited power. To increase the visibility of the bus for passengers and other road users, the front wings and around the entrance were painted white. On the rear panel a white circle about a foot across was painted.

Other steps were taken to make buses less obvious from the air; white or brightly coloured roofs were painted grey and later on in the war many operators adopted liveries of predominantly grey.

Interior lights were dimmed, alternate windows were blocked out or an opaque covering placed over the windows; the latter precaution also lessened the damage from flying glass in the event of a near miss.

Considerable skill was required to drive a laden bus through blacked-out towns, with only very dim lights — and the driver had to find the bus stops.

As the air raids intensified problems became greater. When the warning sounded passengers and crew would retreat to the nearest public shelter; once the all-clear sounded the bus would continue, if the bus was in one piece or the route still passable.

In country areas of Kent buses often had to run the gauntlet of lone raiders on strafing runs. Some buses would have to continue running during the raids; they may not have been able to reach a shelter before the raid started, or they may have been vehicles carrying ARP wardens, rescue teams or troops. Some older single-deckers were converted to ambulances to ferry the injured to hospital. East Kent had thirty such vehicles during the height of the blitz; Maidstone & District converted at least seven vehicles for stretcher carrying.

Bomb damage had reduced London Transport's serviceable fleet to such a level that by October 1940, they had to appeal for provincial buses to assist in the capital. Many vehicles were sent overnight and were in service the next morning, far away from their native towns!

As mentioned earlier East Kent had surplus buses and these were sent about the same time to various operators across the country. Eventually 122 buses from the fleet were dispatched to operators including Aldershot & District, Thames Valley, City of Oxford, East Midlands, Lincolnshire and Caledonian, an erstwhile Scottish operator. Several of these vehicles were dispatched with drivers, particularly those working for armament factories in the Midlands.

Most vehicles retained their East Kent identities, although it is known that Aldershot & District repainted some into their green livery and Thames Valley fitted their own fleet names.

As in the Great War, the loss of male staff into the services resulted in the increased use of female staff generally in the industry, including some who became drivers.

Particularly crippling for the bus operator was a direct hit on a depot. To pre-empt such a disaster Maidstone Corporation dispersed their fleet over several locations each night. Maidstone & District

Standing at Wrotham Square in wartime condition (with masked headlights and white-edged wings) is M & D's CKO998, a 1936 Leyland Titan with lowbridge Weymann bodywork.

unfortunately had not taken such precautions when fifty-one buses were destroyed in a raid on Gillingham Depot on 27th August 1940.

East Kent lost eight buses when the lower depot at Canterbury was destroyed on the night of 31st May 1942 — the loss being reduced by dispersal.

In August 1940 the Whitstable office on the Horsebridge was destroyed, but the worst period was in 1942. On the same night Canterbury depot was hit, the Head Office in Station Road West was also destroyed. Deal, Dover and St Peter's depots also suffered heavy damage around this time.

Later in the war the isolated section of the London Transport trolleybus network, between Woolwich and Dartford, was severely disrupted by a flying bomb hitting the only depot at Bexleyheath. Although many vehicles were badly damaged, all eventually returned to service with repaired or new bodies.

Operations at Dover were particularly difficult as the town was within shelling distance of the French coast. In the town civilian movement was restricted, but there was plenty of demand generated by the military operations. The services were continually disrupted by shelling and blocked roads. Portable bus stops were provided and two double-deckers were converted for use at the various temporary terminals — one as an office, the other a canteen. Two of the ex-Isle of Thanet Daimlers were chosen for this duty as they were non-standard, with highbridge bodies, and both had minor war damage.

At Maidstone the trolleybus system was also disrupted; on 31st October 1940 when Mill Street and Knightrider Street were blocked after bombing, a second set of running wires was installed in Gabriel's Hill and Lower Stone Street to allow two-way running.

By November 1942 the shortage of fuel and rubber for tyres resulted in Government instructions to reduce services. The last buses left at 21.00 from the town centres and did not start until 13.00 on Sundays.

Another fuel conservation measure was the conversion of a number of buses to run on producer gas. The gas was generated on a unit towed behind the bus; power output was only 50% and this limited such vehicles to flat routes. M & D operated sixteen such units in 1943, East Kent had at least five and London Transport also used producer gas units. They were not successful and were soon replaced as petrol supplies increased. Many of M & D's examples were used on Sheppey as a precaution against being cut off from mainland supplies

On the bombed out site of Canterbury depot at the end of the war, is a line of utility Guy Arabs, again showing the camouflage livery carried by all except the most distant bus. (M & D and East Kent Bus Club)

On mobile office duties at Dover is CKP877, a former Isle of Thanet Daimler. (M & D and East Kent Bus Club)

East Kent's JG652 with a producer gas unit; a Leyland Tiger originally an open-topper, it had been rebodied in 1942 following war damage. (M & D and East Kent Bus Club)

should the bridge be hit; thus such buses regularly worked up Minster hill.

Delivery of new buses to operators had virtually ceased by late 1940, with many orders incomplete. East Kent's last ten double-deckers were diverted to Crosville (of Chester) and M & D's last vehicles were some unusual Dodge coaches, which were imported and assembled in this country.

With the fall of France all resources were used on the war effort and bus production was frozen. In late 1941 the Government permitted a number of partly-built buses to be 'unfrozen' and M & D acquired three Bristol single-deckers as a result.

By 1942 many operators were desperate to replace bomb-damaged buses or those permanently requisitioned by the War Department or just to replace worn out vehicles. With the importance of the bus industry to the war effort recognised, limited production recommenced in early 1942.

Three types of double-decker were available: the Guy Arab, the Bristol K type and the Daimler CW type. East Kent and Maidstone Corporation took only the Guy Arab, but Maidstone & District were allocated all three types. The Maidstone Corporation trolleybus fleet was boosted by five Sunbeam vehicles. The only single-decker available was the Bedford OWB. In Kent these vehicles were limited to minor operators — examples being with Newmans of Hythe and The Chartham Bus Company.

All these vehicles were built to the same utility standards, with a single-skin angular body, and no refinements for passenger comfort. No doubt many people will recall the wooden slatted seats fitted to the majority of these vehicles.

As the end of the war neared, the situation generally improved. The supply of utility buses increased, and East Kent vehicles loaned to other operators were returned relieving the chronic shortages. Even so there was still a shortage of vehicles, mostly coaches, in the early years of the peace.

During the bleak years between Dunkirk and the invasion of France the busmen of Kent played an important front line role, bravely and loyally working to keep the necessary services going in adverse conditions.

In 1942 differences between the management of Tilling and BET resulted in a parting of the ways between the two firms. Shares were exchanged so that the various operating companies became Tilling or BET controlled. East Kent, M & D and Southdown all became BET companies, with the Southern Railway holding the balance of shares.

M & D's last Bristol/ECW products before the ban on sales took effect were the 1950 batch of L type saloons. MKN205 was photographed working Tonbridge local 100, which passed under a single-deck only bridge in Priory Road.

(M & D and East Kent Bus Club)

THE POST-WAR YEARS

The post-war years were a boom era for the bus industry, but there were initially problems coping with the demand. Traffic patterns rapidly returned to pre-war levels, but manpower was slow to be released from the services; many of the buses were worn out and new vehicles were in short supply. In 1946 East Kent received just four coaches, but the following year saw considerable deliveries of Dennis and Leyland buses. M & D fared better, although only fifty-five of its 1946 order for seventy-three AEC and Bristol buses had been delivered by the end of the year. Vehicle shortages continued well into the fifties, with both M & D and East Kent having pre-war vehicles extensively rebuilt as semi-chassisless saloons by Beadle's of Dartford, as well as the standard practice of rebodying utility and pre-war buses with new bodies.

The post-war Labour Government nationalised the mainline railway companies from 1st January 1948, which included the Southern Railway's one third share of both East Kent and M & D. Further plans included the compulsory nationalisation of the bus industry; BET put up vigorous opposition, but the Tilling group agreed in September 1948 to sell its bus interests to the British Transport Commission. Another election put paid to further nationalisation moves for some years. One strange result of this was that products of former Tilling group manufacturing companies Bristol and Eastern Coach Works were only available within the BTC. This forced M & D, a regular customer of both firms, to look elsewhere for new vehicles.

The early fifties were the zenith of the bus industry in Kent, with M & D running 900 vehicles for 29 million miles and carrying 165 million passengers in 1950.

Capital reconstruction projects, higher wages and the fuel tax introduced with the 1950 budget all helped to increase costs and this forced East Kent to apply to the Traffic Commissioners for its first ever increase in fares in July 1951; something which has since become a regular feature of the industry, with fare rises often in excess of the general inflation rate. These fare increases together with the growing numbers of cars and televisions resulted in a slow but steady decline in passengers.

Post-war takeovers by M & D included Scout Motor Co, Hastings in May 1951, and Skinner's Luxury Coaches, St Leonard's in August 1953; M & D retained both firms' liveries on some coaches until 1969; the latter operator, it will be recalled, dated from horse bus days. The stage services, but no buses, were acquired from Ashline of Tonbridge in September 1948, becoming 130 to Sevenoaks Weald via Gaza, 131 to Underriver and 132 to Lower Hayesden via Brook Street Estate. From 25th March 1951 Southdown took over Sargent's (formerly East Grinstead Coaches), but the services passed to M & D from 30th September, as they fell within its territory; they were 135 to Edenbridge via Cowden (originally an East Surrey route), 136 to Ashurst Wood and 137 between Edenbridge and Crowborough.

Another M & D Bristol, a 1949 K6A with Weymann bodywork, at Wellington Square, Hastings on the long route to Gravesend.

(M & D and East Kent Bus Club)

East Kent purchased a few small coach operators in the post-war era, such as Saxby of Margate and Sarjent Bros of Cheriton (both in 1953); Sarjent also ran a bus service between Folkestone and Hythe, jointly with East Kent 103/A, and the workings were absorbed on takeover within the existing timetable. The only other bus service to be acquired was the Lydd-Dungeness-New Romney working of Carey Bros of New Romney. This was another long established firm, having run a Folkestone-New Romney horse bus; the takeover date was 31st August 1952.

An important post-war development, reflecting improved living standards, was the operation of extended holiday tours. East Kent's first such programme began in 1949, with M & D following in the early fifties.

For the first decade after the war the stage network remained fairly static, although the growth of new housing estates around almost every town in Kent resulted in the extension of many local routes. Some trunk routes were linked by M & D, like 57 Gravesend-Rochester-Maidstone which was extended to Hastings in place of alternate service 5 journeys in 1949. A pre-war summer only route not restored was 46 which had run from Gravesend to Hastings via West Malling-Wateringbury and Yalding.

Other lengthy routes to evolve were 97 East Grinstead-Tunbridge Wells-Cranbrook/Hawkhurst-Tenterden-Ashford, linked in January 1955, and 122 a four hour plus run between Gravesend and Brighton, joint with Southdown. This commenced from 6th June 1948, with

Southdown's contribution to the Heathfield Scheme included PUF639, a 1956 Guy Arab/Park Royal.

Another Southdown vehicle, RUF51, a Beadle bodied Leyland Tiger Cub, stops at Rye on the South Coast Express.

22, formerly Gravesend-Borough Green-Tunbridge Wells-Crowborough, reduced to Gravesend-Vigo short-workings. Co-ordination with BET neighbour Southdown was further increased from 2nd June 1955, with the introduction of the Heathfield Scheme.

All the trunk routes at Heathfield became jointly operated on a complicated roster that resulted in some buses spending several nights away from their own depot and some journeys being worked by each company's vehicle on alternate days; routes ran every two hours, but by changing at Heathfield an hourly facility between all points was available. They were 18 Hawkhurst-Brighton, 152 Tunbridge Wells-Hastings, 180 Hastings-Brighton, 190 Hawkhurst-Eastbourne, 191 Tunbridge Wells-Eastbourne and 192 Uckfield-Eastbourne.

The lower shed at Canterbury was rebuilt during 1946/7, allowing the release of the upper shed for the coachworks again, which had been located at Faversham since the destructive air-raid in 1942. Post-war shortages meant other repairs were slow to be done and Dover depot was not fully repaired until 1955. The same year saw the opening of a new bus station at Folkestone, and in 1956 the original cramped bus station adjoining the Westgate Towers at Canterbury was closed and services moved to a larger site at St George's Lane at the other end of the City. Many other premises were extended and modernised and a new depot was opened in 1960 at Ore, Hastings replacing an old shed acquired in 1948; the small Whitstable shed was closed in 1950, followed by the one-bus depot at Wye in 1952.

M & D also had a major post-war programme of infrastructure improvements; these included a new shed at Ashford and a complete rebuild giving increased capacity at Borough Green, both in 1954. A new garage combined with a bus station was opened at Hawkhurst in 1950 and a third shed added at Hastings in 1954. Tunbridge Wells was extended in 1954 including a new staff canteen and Sittingbourne received a complete reconstruction in 1960. New depots were opened at Edenbridge in 1955 and Tonbridge in 1961. A combined depot and bus station was opened at Leysdown in 1958, mainly to deal with traffic on the E14 and E19 coach routes from London, which were then carrying 50,000 passengers a season; a second bus station in Maidstone was opened in 1951 at the other end of Palace Avenue — this was known as Lower Stone Street Bus Station and the original site, to avoid confusion, became known as Mill Street Bus Station.

The heavy flooding of the North Kent coast on 31st January 1953 resulted in East Kent providing forty-four buses on substitute rail service between Faversham and Birchington for a month while the track was restored, and a further twenty vehicles were used for many months to convey workers on sea defence works.

The first 36 foot saloon for M & D was S1 (984TKO); it was an AEC Reliance with a 54-seat Willowbrook body; this view shows it leaving Canterbury Bus Station when nearly new.   (M & D and East Kent Bus Club)

Rising costs and falling custom resulted in the companies looking for economies in the mid-fifties, the most important of which was the arrival of modern underfloor engined saloons seating around forty, that were worked one-man-operated on mainly rural routes. To speed up this process East Kent also had a number of rear entrance Dennis Lancets rebuilt for OMO working.

1956 saw the Suez Crisis necessitating fuel rationing from 17th December, with the Hydrocarbon Oil Duties Act allowing operators to increase fares to cover the higher fuel prices. From this date East Kent suspended four routes entirely and some 5% of stage work was withdrawn. From 30th December, after the Christmas rush, coach operation was cut by 50%; from the same day M & D made similar cuts to its services. During the first few months of 1957 the fuel supply improved, but some of the timings withdrawn were never replaced, and others served as a pattern for later permanent reductions.

At this stage it is useful to review the state of the industry; trunk routes and town services were operated by double-deckers seating around fifty-six passengers, although those with sunken side gangways for working under low bridges sat about fifty-three. East Kent had always specified lowbridge vehicles until 1951, although few such obstructions were found in their area. M & D had always had a mixture of both types, despite having more than its fair share of low bridges at West Malling, Bexhill, and the now removed one at Horsmonden to cite only the most infamous — several buses having lost

The original Hastings trolleybuses were replaced during the 1940s; one of the replacement vehicles was BDY804, a 1946 Sunbeam/Park Royal.
(M & D and East Kent Bus Club)

Trolleybus replacement buses were Leyland Atlanteans; 53DKT was one of the fourteen lowbridge examples and was photographed outside Bexhill depot. (M & D and East Kent Bus Club)

their tops over the years! Frequencies were high, for example Tonbridge to Tunbridge Wells had ten buses an hour in 1958 (now six) or the Thanet trunk routes running every six minutes (now every fifteen minutes). Some routes still had increased frequencies on Saturdays, like 101 Tunbridge Wells-Leigh or 17 between Chatham and Cliffe, but this requirement was declining rapidly.

Many rural routes still had a frequent service, including Sunday operation; four Sunday runs were provided on 43 Sittingbourne-Frinsted with three more journeys as far as Milstead. This route also boasted two late trips on Saturday evenings and in 1958 it was still conductor operated using older style single-deckers.

Buses were limited to 30 mph (except on the new motorways) until 1961, when the speed was increased to 40 mph. Two other important changes in legislation resulted in the length limit for two-axle double-deckers of 30 foot in 1958, and in 1962 36 foot long single-deckers were allowed that could seat fifty-three.

The Hastings trolleybuses were taken into the main M & D fleet in 1957 and ceased operation on 31st May 1959. They were replaced by new generation rear engined Leyland Atlanteans, seating seventy-eight, although fourteen lowbridge examples for use under Sackville Arch at Bexhill sat seventy-three. These vehicles cost about £6,250 each, compared with £3,500 for the front-engined AEC Regent that East Kent purchased, but they proved to be a good investment. The final trolleybus routes were T2, a very rural circular via Ore, St

Helens, Baldslow and Silverhill running every forty-five minutes, T6 running every six minutes from Ore to Silverhill with alternate trips to Hollington, T8 Park Cross Road to Cooden via Bexhill and Bulverhythe, and T11 from St Helens to Silverhill/Hollington via Old Town and St Leonards.

Small cuts in rural routes were being made in the late fifties. For example, 23rd March 1958 saw 123 Maidstone-Stockbury and 92 Wadhurst-Crowborough withdrawn and 107 Tunbridge Wells-Chiddingstone lose its Tuesday/Thursday operation leaving only the Saturday service. From the same date the East Grinstead extension of 97 was cut back to Tunbridge Wells, being replaced by 93 Tunbridge Wells-Penshurst-Edenbridge running back to Tunbridge Wells via Hever and Cowden, with 135 Edenbridge-East Grinstead diverted via Stick Hill instead of Hever. East Kent withdrew 111 Hythe local and 104 Folkestone-Aylesham from 10th May 1959.

New routes continued to be introduced to serve the ever growing housing estates, like M & D 123 Tunbridge Wells to Southborough, Manor Road Estate introduced on 13th February 1961. The Beeching cuts to the Kentish railway network resulted in some replacement bus routes being introduced; 92 Hawkhurst to Paddock Wood from 12th June 1961 and with effect from 3rd December 1961 136 from Gravesend to Allhallows, but such routes attracted even fewer passengers than the branch trains, and they lasted no longer than the subsidies paid by the railways as a condition of the closures.

The Atlanteans had a long life; 558LKP, a 1960 example was restored to M & D's traditional dark green and cream livery in 1980. It was pictured in Maidstone on 28th January 1984, its last day in revenue earning service and it is now retained by the company as a preserved bus.

The opening of the Dartford Tunnel resulted in improved coach links between Kent and Essex for the 1964 season; they were jointly operated with Eastern National (a former Tilling fleet, now part of the nationalised Transport Holding Company) and marketed under the Dartford Tunnel Coachways banner. Route X33 provided a Maidstone to Walton and a Colchester to Hastings facility, X40 Gillingham-Great Yarmouth, X32 Folkestone-Clacton and X34 Ramsgate-Clacton. These replaced earlier facilities via the Tilbury Ferry. Later, to partially replace the withdrawn London Transport service through the tunnel, Eastern National introduced a limited-stop route 402 between Southend and Dartford (since the 1980 Transport Act this route has been extended to Victoria over former Green Line mileage). Another new facility to start in 1964 was MX8 from Northampton to Ramsgate, worked by United Counties, but nominally joint with East Kent; this route also used the new tunnel.

The University of Kent at Canterbury provided a fresh traffic flow, with service 32 from the bus station to the University introduced in 1965.

January 1966 saw extensive revisions to services at Hastings; the country routes, that previously terminated at Wellington Square, were diverted to Queens Road Coach Station or to cover certain local routes. At the same time 57 Gravesend-Hastings was withdrawn south of Maidstone and converted to OMO.

A new East Kent service, 142, commenced on 6th March 1967 between Lade and Appledore, replacing trains on the New Romney branch.

As buses increased in size there became various restrictions on certain routes that could not be worked by all vehicles, some locations even requiring special buses. East Kent's ten small Bedford VASs arrived in 1967 to replace the remaining Dennis Falcon saloons on restricted rural routes. Two rail bridges were too low for modern underfloor-engined saloons. At Ashford the Newtown Road bridge resulted in the retention of a pair of Dennis Lancets beyond their normal span, until two Bedford VASs were released from other work to replace them in 1969. It is interesting to note that when these buses were replaced in 1975 by some special low and narrow Bristol LHSs only four vehicles were needed to cover the restricted routes; although this did prove a little optimistic as many journeys were lost due to no suitable bus being available.

The other example at Priory Road, Tonbridge on the local route to Dowgates Close, was not quite so low and some early AEC Reliances (with roof vents shut) could pass; here the problem was solved by diverting the service via Pembury Road to avoid the bridge. In 1960 M & D purchased fifteen Albion Nimbus 30-seaters to work lightly loaded routes. In 1962 some were drafted into Hastings to replace elderly Bristols working routes over the narrow Castle Hill, but high loadings and poor vehicle availability resulted in their replacement in 1963 by ten narrow AEC Reliances seating forty-two. In 1967, following the demolition of some old houses, the road was widened permitting the use of normal buses.

In 1962 East Kent purchased three AEC Bridgemasters, which were used exclusively on Dover local 129 under the 14 foot high bridge in Coombe Valley Road. This route was converted to single-deck in 1970.

Among the services to use the Dartford Tunnel is Eastern National 402; this 1975 view shows BNO102B, a Bristol RELH/ECW at Dartford.

CFN151 was one of the East Kent Dennis Lancets rebuilt to front entrance for one-man-operation; it is here seen on Ashford local 124, which passed under the Newtown Road bridge.   (M & D and East Kent Bus Club)

M & D continued to buy rear engined buses, switching to Daimler Fleetlines for double-deckers in 1963, which, by use of dropped centre axles, could be bodied to a low height without resorting to sunken side gangways; in 1968 some of these buses became the first OMO double-deckers in the area.

We end this era with the traditional network and scale of operations largely intact, although many routes were now driver-only operated and some thinning of evening and Sunday working was evident. Overall profits were declining, for example 60% of East Kent's stage routes were running at a loss in 1966 (compared with 47% in 1955), but profits from the main trunk routes still allowed cross-subsidisation of rural routes and a small dividend for the share-holders.

THE NATIONAL BUS COMPANY

The Labour Government of the mid sixties introduced many changes in the transport industry, including nationalisation of the remaining large bus companies, which were embodied in the Transport Act, 1968. Initially BET objected, but on 14th March 1968 it sold its bus interests to the Transport Holding Company (successor to the BTC) for £35m; BET had diversified into other fields and also ran bus fleets in many commonwealth countries, and it continues today as a large international group.

The Act duly became law on 28th November and the National Bus Company came into existence on 1st January 1969; exactly a year later under the Transport (London) Act, 1969 the Country Bus and Coach departments of London Transport passed to the NBC. These became the London Country Bus Services Ltd, based at the old East Surrey address at Bell Street, Reigate. This was part of a plan to put London Transport under the control of the GLC, and to improve the alignment of LT and GLC there have subsequently been some minor territory changes between LT and LCBS. The 'Polo' shaped operating area of LCBS has caused considerable management problems, and its fragmentation, resulting in M & D acquiring the Kentish part, has often been rumoured but has never come to fruition. Nevertheless there have been several exchanges of operations between the two firms, and also between M & D and East Kent. NBC headquarters imposed various management structure changes, and there was a general move to unify East Kent and M & D into one company. In 1972 the late Len Higgins became Chief General Manager of both East Kent and M & D (and also Southdown for a while) and after many years of centralisation on Canterbury for headquarters functions, the M & D head office and central works were finally closed in 1981. Despite the registration of the name of Northdown the final merger never took place, as there was a drastic change of policy in 1983.

The 1968 Act also gave financial help to the industry in the form of 50% grants towards the cost of new buses for stage services and the provision for councils to pay subsidies to cover losses on socially desirable services. Despite increasing support (for example Kent CC paid £155,000 in 1974/5, £286,000 in the following financial year and about £½m in 1976/7) extensive reductions in services were necessary, along with 'higher than inflation' fare rises. These cuts, along with the NBC reorganisation resulted in the closure of many of the company's depots and enquiry offices.

LCBS had many problems in the seventies; it inherited a fleet of elderly or unreliable buses and it lost access to LT's Aldenham Works, especially important for Routemaster overhauls. All this came to a head during 1975, when delays in delivery of new vehicles and failures of the existing ones were resulting in lost mileage; to combat this many hired and second-hand buses were drafted in. Those working in Kent were AEC Regents from Eastbourne Borough at Swanley, Leyland Titans from Maidstone Borough at Dartford and Bristol coaches from Royal Blue at Dunton Green. By 1977 the position had been eased considerably by new buses and the opening of LCBS's works at Crawley.

A lighter green with yellow relief was adopted by LCBS as their new livery, with a logo that was a modified version of the LT roundel; this proved short lived as the NBC liveries began to appear in 1972. These were poppy red (East Kent) or grass green (M & D and LCBS) with a white band on stage buses and allover white on coaches; dual-purpose vehicles, including Green Line coaches, were white with the fleet colour. Block capital fleet names were used along with the 'double N' symbol.

For a while it looked as if the vehicle side would become very boring, with Bristol VRTs and Leyland Atlanteans double-deckers, Leyland-National saloons and AEC Reliance and Leyland Leopard coaches forming most of the orders. Salvation came in several forms, like overall advert and marketing liveries, various second-hand purchases and the choice of M & D to undertake vehicle trials for the NBC between the VRT, the Volvo Ailsa and the Metro-Scania in 1976 and again in 1980 between the Dennis Dominator and the Metrobus.

East Kent took its first rear-engined double-deckers in 1969 and they were soon used for OMO operation. Some AEC Regents were converted to OMO but, except for the full front 1959 batch, they were most unsuitable and they soon reverted to other work; some were sent to M & D in exchange for both OMO saloons and double-deckers and to further speed OMO conversions thirty Leyland Leopards were acquired from Southdown in 1971.

Leaving Dartford Depot is 479CLT, a former Green Line AEC Routemaster about to take up service on a Dartford local.

One of the buses hired by London Country to cover vehicle shortages was DHC649 an AEC Regent from Eastbourne Borough Council; the picture was taken in Orpington High Street.

Part of the problem was the unreliability of the rear-engined AEC Merlin; this example in the new NBC livery was working at Gravesend.

M & D's JKK177E, a Leyland Panther/Willowbrook, takes fuel at Gravesend depot on the night before closure.

At Westerham in January 1982 is M & D LJH254L (an ex-Dengate Leyland Leopard/Plaxton) about to work to Dormansland on service 328.

KFN217, an East Kent AEC Reliance/Weymann of 1955 about to leave Rye for Camber; at this stage it was in fact working on hire to M & D.

In December 1977 LCBS began selling its Routemaster fleet back to London Transport; the last examples were at Northfleet and Swanley and survived until March 1980. One was preserved by LCBS and was used to work 477 Dartford-Orpington on 13th March 1981, the last day crew operation on this route and indeed the whole of LCBS, on a regular basis.

Gravesend local routes were revised on 30th October 1976, when M & D 307/8 were extended to Painters Ash, Coldharbour and Northfleet replacing LCBS 498 and LCBS 480 continued to Valley Drive, with 487 working to Hever Court in lieu of M & D 306/5 respectively.

This arrangement proved to be temporary for on 1st April 1978 extensive service cuts in North Kent resulted in the closure of M & D's Gravesend depot, with M & D 307/8 passing to LCBS as 497/8; other M & D operations were transferred to Borough Green or Gillingham.

Other withdrawals the same day included 401 south of Eynsford Station (leaving passengers to Sevenoaks to the railway), and Green Line 719 to Wrotham, although a limited replacement 729 was provided at peak hours running through to Borough Green. This passed to M & D operation, becoming 929, from 19th July 1980 with M & D 55 Sevenoaks-Seal-Kemsing passing to LCBS, which was integrated with their existing route via Otford (421) as circular routes 457/67. An interesting service which ran on summer Sundays during 1979 and 1980 was ramblers bus 418, which ran a figure of eight from Sevenoaks via Toys Hill and Brasted on the western loop and Godden Green, Ightham and Kemsing on the eastern leg.

LCBS operations through Edenbridge were reduced to one route (485 East Grinstead to Westerham) after the cuts of August 1975, and from 27th January 1979 it omitted to serve the Troy Town area of Edenbridge in favour of M & D's new local service 240. With the closure of East Grinstead depot on the last day of 1981 485 was withdrawn, with M & D providing a partial replacement with 238 Westerham to Dormansland. LCBS made a small return to the town with a new ramblers bus 452 Sevenoaks-Ide Hill-Hever-Penshurst-Sevenoaks in 1984.

M & D introduced the Eden Valley Village Bus scheme (with council support) on 19th March 1979 using a special liveried Ford saloon. The local route became E1, with E2 breaking new ground with a Monday shopping run to Bromley and E3/4 providing shopping facilities to Sevenoaks via Toys Hill on Wednesdays and Ide Hill on Fridays. E2 attracted little custom and from 14th October 1979 it was replaced by E5 to Tonbridge.

The Green Line routes 704/5 lost their cross-London link with Windsor in April 1979, 704 becoming 706 as a result; further cuts from 21st April 1981 resulted in 706 being truncated at Bromley North on most journeys and diverted via Weald to cover 454 Fort Halstead-Sevenoaks-Tonbridge, which was reduced to peak hours only. The most recent M & D penetration into LCBS area came on 7th September 1982 with an extension of a single trip on school bus 203 Tonbridge-Weald to Knockholt.

The first of the route exchanges between East Kent and M & D took place on 7th September 1969, when the former Timpson services 127/8 to Pett and Pett Level became M & D 171 & 170 respectively; East Kent's depot at Ore was closed as a result.

The long route 122 Brighton-Gravesend was split at Tunbridge Wells with effect from 5th July 1970; the southern leg became 219, and through working of Southdown buses beyond Tunbridge Wells

In exact reverse to the traditional operating pattern an M & D Leyland-National prepares to work to Whitstable from Faversham, while in the background an East Kent example is on the Ashford service. This view was taken on 5th March 1977, the day before this section of Court Street was closed for pedestrianisation.

ceased. The Heathfield Scheme workings were discontinued from 25th April 1971, when service levels were reduced and some routes were truncated at Heathfield, thus ending Southdown operation to Hawkhurst.

1971 was a year of many cuts in services, many roads lost evening and Sunday journeys, one-man-operation increased dramatically (including with double-deckers) and some depots such as Borough Green and Sheerness became 100% OMO during the year. A sample of route losses during the year includes 67 Canterbury-Maidstone curtailed at Charing from 7th March and becoming worked solely by East Kent; it connected with route 10 Folkestone-Maidstone which also had a reduced timetable. From 26th September 10 was further revised with diversions of some runs via Brabourne/Lympne replacing facilities on rural routes. 30th May saw East Kent 18 Canterbury-Folkestone via Stelling Minnis withdrawn south of Lyminge, where it connected with service 17 via the Elham Valley.

4th July saw a major cut in rural services in mid-Kent with 2 Ashford-Biddenden cut back to Smarden, 49 Ashford-Headcorn withdrawn, 12a losing its Pluckley-Charing section and two routes from Faversham, 28 and 60, losing their twice weekly extension over the North Downs to Lenham. More cuts followed from 19th September when service 6 from Maidstone was truncated at Goudhurst, losing the legs to Hawkhurst and Kilndown; service 24 Maidstone-Horsmonden was also reduced, with the two bus depot at Horsmonden closing at the same time.

East Kent's Faversham depot closed on 3rd July 1971, and its small allocation moved to the M & D garage. Three weeks later East Kent locals at Ashford were reorganised as services 501-10, including replacement of M & D's short workings to Kennington on route 11 to Faversham. Town routes at Dover were also numbered into the new series (becoming 301-8/10) from 26th September, all being OMO, and this was followed by Deal locals being renumbered 381-5 from 26th March 1972.

East Kent routes 2 and 112 between Rye and Ashford were reduced from 3rd January 1972, but as a partial replacement M & D 73 (Tenterden-Appledore) was extended to Rye via Stone and Iden. Control of East Kent's Rye operation passed to M & D from 25th March 1973, with fourteen vehicles passing on loan to M & D (four of which were later acquired, and the remainder returned over the next fifteen months); all routes became joint services, bringing M & D service buses into fresh territory, including on a truncated service 62 between Hastings and Dover.

In the reverse direction East Kent took over at Ashford from 6th May 1973, gaining service 71 to Lenham Heath, an additional car on service 10, and part of the workings to Faversham on route 11.

Rising fares and service reductions resulted in several local councils introducing free bus services and/or fare tokens for old age pensioners. The first of the now familiar advert liveried buses appeared in 1972, giving a useful source of revenue.

To encourage days out by bus East Kent introduced the 'day anywhere' Wanderbus ticket in 1970 (later adopted by M & D and Southdown) and in 1972 the first of the zonal season tickets were promoted.

Typifying the National Express image is PVB801S, an East Kent Leyland Leopard/Duple in National white livery, shown arriving at Dover on 008 from London.

Not all service changes were negative as many town routes were extended into new housing estates. In particular the vast housing developments south and east of the Medway Towns resulted in some new routes, including to Maidstone. The first of these was 116, a limited stop workers facility from Wigmore and Rainham, which started on 13th December 1971. It was followed a few months later by 110 running every two hours from Chatham via Walderslade. After an application by an independent for a similar route, services 49/A/B commenced on 1st April 1973 from Farthing Corner and Rainham to Maidstone via Bredhurst and Boxley Hill. Because of narrow roads East Kent Bedford VASs were hired for the service initially, but subsequent alterations have allowed full-sized buses to be used.

October 1973 saw the introduction of two new numbering schemes; firstly on the seventh of the month M & D started to phase in a new area number scheme with Gravesend and Swale services becoming 3xx numbers, Tunbridge Wells area routes 2xx and Hastings/East Sussex 4xx numbers. The end of the month saw the National Express services given a country-wide numbering scheme, East Kent's London services became 001-008, the South Coast Express became 026, M & D operated routes became 031-054 and the Dartford Tunnel routes became 122-136.

M & D took over the remaining three East Kent operators at Faversham from 30th December 1973; services becoming numbered in a 6xx sequence. As a result M & D acquired the Chilham route (661 ex 31), and a share of 637/8 (ex 37/8) to Whitstable and Herne Bay.

From 2nd June 1974 a new route between Hastings and Rye, 414, was introduced linking the former Hastings to Pett Level and Rye to Winchelsea Beach services; this was followed from 7th July by the renumbering of the other M & D numbers into the 4xx series. A further East Sussex scheme from 20th April 1975 included new links between Rye and Battle as routes 408/9, a coastal service between Rye and Eastbourne (499) jointly with Southdown and the diversion of more local routes via the railway station at Hastings.

Heading for the entrance ramp of Chatham Bus Station is M & D KJD119P, a former London Transport Daimler Fleetline/Park Royal; its dome fleet number is clearly visible.

Representing the second phase of the NBC vehicle tests is FKM303V, one of the Dennis Dominators with Willowbrook bodywork; it was photographed at Davis Estate, Chatham.

Leaving the William Harvey Hospital at Ashford in November 1979 is PNU388R, a Bristol LH/ECW hired from Trent to work the service initially; note the lack of passengers!

More major changes came on 14th December 1975; at Chatham routes were recast to use the new Pentagon Bus Station (although it was not fully opened until the following March). Closed-circuit TV is used here for control and this has resulted in the large roof fleet numbers carried by the fleet to aid identification. One feature of the revised network was the extension of the majority of buses terminating at Davis Estate to Walderslade via the new link road; the same date also saw a revised and renumbered pattern of service on the London and Ashford Roads out of Maidstone.

Other important revisions in the Medway Towns came from 14th August 1977 with the opening of Chatham Railway Station Interchange, when alterations included the running of new limited stop routes for commuters from Lordswood (766) and Walderslade (784). The new out-of-town Hempstead Valley Shopping Centre was central to further revisions in the Medway Towns from 15th October 1978, when several routes were revised to serve the new centre, including the Maidstone via Boxley Hill route now numbered 131. It has become an important focal point for routes serving the ever growing estates at Hempstead and Wigmore and from 22nd January 1984 included new routes from Eastcourt (146) and Luton via a new link road (146/7).

A Folkestone and Romney Marsh scheme from 1st August 1976 gave East Kent its first stage service to Tenterden with 814 a Thursday only shopping run from New Romney. The original Mill Street Bus Station in Maidstone was closed on 5th September 1976; it had been rebuilt with a rear exit in 1969 to cope with the one-way system. All routes were transferred to Lower Stone Street, which had been rebuilt in a saw-tooth layout to increase capacity. The same day a new depot for East Kent was opened at Cobbs Wood, Ashford. This was planned to coincide with more cuts at Ashford and Tunbridge Wells, that were delayed until 3rd October: 97 from Tunbridge Wells became 297 and was cut back to Tenterden and the Cranbrook-Hawkhurst section was also withdrawn, the Ashford to Tenterden section became 400. East Kent took a larger share of 11 to Faversham (now 666) and in return M & D gained an operator on 603 (ex 3) between Faversham and Canterbury.

Just as service numbers were being combined into one series, so the East Kent buses were given fleet numbers in the M & D system from May 1977; prior to this they had used the numerals of the registration for identification.

1977 also saw plans for a countywide network of 7xx limited-stop routes, for which twenty coach-seated Leyland-Nationals were ordered; most plans fell through but 729 joint with Southdown, between Tunbridge Wells and Brighton ran from 30th January 1977, with 219/29 running only to Crowborough as a result.

At Faversham a new hourly local circular was introduced from 13th November 1977 as 676, giving several areas of the town a much improved service, although it must be recorded that further cuts took place in the rural routes at the same time.

More cuts at Thanet from 2nd October included wider headways on some trunk roads and this was followed by rationalisation at Dover with effect from 8th January 1978, which featured renumbering the town routes from the 3xx series to 5xx numbers to avoid clashes with M & D routes; country routes also lost their traditional numbers in favour of new 5xx ones.

The North Kent revisions of 1st April 1978, already mentioned with respect to LCBS, also resulted in revised services in the West Malling area. West Peckham lost its bus service as the 70 group was diverted to the new Lunsford Park Estate. The Snodland extension was increased, replacing the indirect route to Maidstone by service 150 from Gillingham to Maidstone via West Malling, which was generally reduced to a Gillingham-West Malling service with odd extensions to Mereworth.

Another major scheme for East Sussex on 21st April 1978 resulted in 12 Maidstone to Hastings being diverted at Tenterden to Rye, absorbing 402 over that section. A through link between Ashford and Hastings was achieved by extending service 400 over former 12 mileage. At Rye the local service to Rye Harbour was withdrawn and covered by double-running of buses on the coastal run to Hastings. Further revisions the next year allowed Hastings Brook Street depot to lose its stage services to Silverhill from 3rd September; Brook Street lasted a while for coach operation before its final closure. Just prior to this on 29th July the Heathfield outstation had also closed.

The opening of a new area hospital at Ashford resulted in the running of the KCC inspired William Harvey Hospital Bus from 2nd July 1979; it was worked by a Bristol LHS hired from Trent pending the arrival of a Ford midibus in a special fawn livery. Routes ran on a one or two days a week basis as 801 to Lydd Camp, 802 to Elham, 803 to Biddenden, 804 to Hastingleigh and 805 to Lydd-on-Sea. Loadings proved non-existent and from 4th November it was cut to 801/2 to Lydd via various marsh villages.

Thus in little over a decade the industry had changed dramatically, with operating areas redrawn, services restructured and renumbered, with many losing their traditional identity to the confusion of the travelling public. Added to this one-way and pedestrianisation schemes have affected most towns, often increasing journey times or reducing access to central areas. Some routes had gained obscure diversions to cover withdrawals on other services, or works and school requirements; the later being a major peak commitment with the increasing centralisation of schools. Overriding all this were the cuts in services, and the poor financial situation of the operators.

But worse was still to come . . .

An East Kent Leyland Royal Tiger/Park Royal coach tests the loading ramp on an early RoRo ferry at Calais in 1953.

(M & D and East Kent Bus Club)

Displaying the Europabus livery at Victoria Coach Station is East Kent's MJG285, an AEC Reliance with Beadle (of Dartford) bodywork.

(M & D and East Kent Bus Club)

CONTINENTAL SERVICES

Kent's proximity to the continent has generated much business for the local operators, especially East Kent. As early as 1930 East Kent advertised coach and steamer trips to Ostende and staff at M & D's Dartford depot were able to take one of the company's coaches to Folkestone for a day trip on the Boulogne steamer.

It was not until the 1950s that coaches regularly crossed the channel, when the first of the roll-on roll-off ferries were introduced. Since then there has been a phenomenal growth in this traffic for day trips, holiday packages and even international express coach services. Over a decade ago it was the continental tourists who were invading our shops and Canterbury Bus Station was often full of vehicles bringing trippers off the boats at Dover and Folkestone — double-deckers were popular on this work! One of the largest jobs was on 1st May 1967, when 1,500 Belgian tourists were taken round Kent in thirty-five coaches, Today the flow is in the other direction, with the 'bottle run' to Calais hypermarket attracting many English coaches.

Between 1953 and 1970 East Kent operated the English section of the Europabus network — and from 1961 coaches in a special pale blue livery were used. Three trips a day ran from Victoria to Dover Docks, connecting with the ferry. With Ro-Ro ferry operation coaches now work through and are currently supplied by National Travel.

1955 saw the inauguration of the Skyways London to Paris coach/ air link, with East Kent providing the coach service from Victoria to Lympne Airport. Special liveried coaches were also a feature of this link from 1956 until 1971, when Skyways became bankrupt and the service ceased. A similar, but short-lived facility was provided for Silver City Services at Lydd and Manston.

The cross channel ferries have traditionally been served (and indeed owned) by the railways, but the development of Dover Eastern Docks has given East Kent much local work. Again there has been a tremendous increase in this type of operation, starting in 1968 with just one bus conveying foot-passengers from the terminal to the Sea-link ships, to the present position with nearly twenty vehicles in various contract liveries plus the use of standard red buses at peak times.

In 1970 the Seaspeed (BR Hovercraft) contract began between Priory Station and the Hoverport in the Eastern Docks; a special livery of blue was used and around the same time a similar scheme appeared for the Sealink service. These contracts initially gave a life extension to some of the fine Dennis Lancet UF coaches, but more recently as the demand has increased some double-deckers have appeared (the first being in 1976 with three Regents in Sealink colours), as have a number of saloons that for various reasons were not successful on intensive stage service work; most notable of these

Townsend Thoresen Ferries operate this ex London Transport AEC Swift, seen at Dover Eastern Docks in July 1981.

East Kent operate this former Southdown Daimler Fleetline/Northern Counties on the P & O Ferries contract at Dover, and it was photographed at the Priory Station. (M & D and East Kent Bus Club)

Leaving the same location is BEH143H, a Daimler Fleetline/Alexander acquired from Potteries for the Hoverport service.

are the ex-M & D Fleetlines. In 1978 increased Seaspeed requirements, following the opening of the new Hoverport by Dover Pier and the introduction of the stretched hovercraft, resulted in the purchase of five Daimler Fleetline saloons from Potteries.

P & O began a ferry service from Dover in 1976 and a similar contract is operated by East Kent for their sailings. Initially a single AEC Regent was in P & O colours, but currently there are three ex-Southdown double-deck Fleetlines in their light blue, black and white livery.

The third ferry operator at Dover, Townsend-Thoresen, has always operated its own vehicles on its shuttle service. Two ex-East Kent Regents were used from 1972-77, when some former London Transport AEC Merlins arrived (AML602/5H); these were later joined by AEC Swift AML97H and Fleetlines MLK646/53L from the same source and all five remain in use. Until June 1978 the service ran only between the Docks and their office in Camden Crescent, but from this date it was extended to serve the Priory Station.

In March 1969 Hoverlloyd opened the Hoverport at Pegwell Bay, with East Kent providing a connecting facility from London and also from Ramsgate Station. In 1972 three coaches were painted in a special red and white livery to work this service; in 1976 two more modern vehicles were given the Hoverlloyd contract livery, but with a reorganisation within the NBC, operation was transferred to National Travel South East at Catford; the two coaches in contract colours were also moved in exchange for two white coaches going the other way. This was to be a short-lived arrangement, as the contract was lost to Wallace Arnold Coaches of Leeds, who operated it from their London depot, again with coaches in a special livery.

The Ramsgate Station link was quickly discontinued by East Kent, although it was operated for a while by Eastonways, a local coach firm.

In 1982 Hoverlloyd merged with Seaspeed to form Hoverspeed, with the majority of crossings using Dover. The Pegwell Bay Hoverport was totally closed by 1983, with all operations transferred to Dover, including the express coach link operated by Wallace Arnold. East Kent have continued to work the local shuttle at Dover, with ex-Southdown Fleetline double-deckers in the new Hoverspeed contract livery.

During 1978/9 M & D operated one coach in a special livery for a London to Sheerness service in connection with the Olau-Line sailings. From January 1980 this traffic was lost to British Rail, although M & D provides a connecting run from the Station to the Docks.

From 1978 to 1981, both M & D and East Kent operated coaches in Townsend-Thoresen livery for day tours to France; in 1980/1 there was a similar operation for P & O Landtours. Since 1981 Townsend-Thoresen have operated their own coaches from a depot at Larkfield; the current fleet includes ADV 142-6Y, Volvos with rather exotic bodywork by the Italian firm Padane.

At Ramsgate Harbour in 1959 is BJG472, a 1945 Guy Arab in the reversed livery used for open-toppers.　　　(M & D and East Kent Bus Club)

Resting at Sheerness Bus Station between journeys is OT8, M & D's sole open-top Bristol.
　　　　　　　(M & D and East Kent Bus Club)

OPEN-TOP SERVICES

With the coastal location of this area it is not surprising that open-top services have played an important role. Passengers of early buses had little choice but to enjoy the fresh air, even during mid-winter, but by the thirties most buses were built fully enclosed.

M & D were early to realise the marketability of open-top buses to the holidaymaker, as six of their 1939 delivery of Leyland Titan were built as open-toppers (the last buses built without roofs in the country), which were used at Hastings. No doubt the lack of roofs was unwelcome during the war years, but subsequently they proved popular on the various seafront routes at Hastings and sometimes made longer runs to Rye or Battle. They were briefly joined for the 1947 and 1948 seasons by an older Titan which had lost its roof under Sackville Arch at Bexhill.

In 1951 four 1934 Dennis Ace saloons were converted to open-top to work a Hastings town tour; these were replaced in 1958 by the conversion of three 1946 AEC Regals, two of which continue to work this service today with Hastings & District.

The eight open-top Hastings trolleybuses had been replaced in 1940, but number 3 (DY4965) had survived as a service vehicle. In June 1953 it was restored to service specially decorated for the Coronation; subsequently it was decorated to record the connection with the Battle of Hastings and gained the nickname of 'Happy Harold', appearing each summer to run between the Fishmarket and the Bathing Pool. When the trolleybuses were withdrawn M & D took the unprecedented step of converting this veteran to diesel using a Commer TS3 engine and a conventional gearbox, running in this form each summer from 1960 to 1968, when it was stored. In 1975 all the decorative lighting and hoardings were removed and the vehicle restored to original condition (except the engine!) by M & D. In 1980 it passed to Hastings Borough Council for continued preservation and publicity use. Since 1976 the author has had the privilege of being one of the regular drivers for this unique vehicle.

Latterly an open-topper worked from Sheerness on normal routes: in 1965 all of M & D's double-deck examples were withdrawn without replacement, leaving just the three single-deckers, one of which was sent to Sheerness for a Round The Island Tour. This ceased in 1969, and with only two vehicles being adequate for the Hastings service, the third one was withdrawn in 1970.

A further saloon, an AEC Reliance, was converted to work a new service 458 West St Leonards to Hastings Country Park in 1975 and

Standing at the Pegwell Bay Hoverport is PFN870, one of the 1959 AEC Regent/Park Royals with full-front bodywork converted in 1972 to open-top form. (M & D and East Kent Bus Club)

The current East Kent open-top fleet includes XKO72A, a former M & D Leyland Atlantean originally registered 572RKJ (now transferred to a coach); this July 1984 view was taken at Joss Bay.

1976: in 1977 it was allocated to 413 Hastings to Fairlight, which proved to be its last year in service. For the 1984 season Hastings & District introduced an hourly seafront service, using a double-decker.

East Kent's last buses built without roofs were all withdrawn or rebodied by the latter years of the war and it was not until 1959 that four utility Guy Arabs were deroofed, with two more following in 1960. These all worked from Westwood depot on special routes 56 Minnis Bay to Palm Bay and 69 Winterstoke Crescent to Cliffsend; this later worked from Broadstairs Front to Cliffsend.

In 1962 a 1951 Guy Arab lost its roof in an accident and was converted to open-top, allowing one bus to be employed on route 44 between Herne Bay and Reculver.

For the 1968 season it was decided that the spare bus at Westwood would be sent to Folkestone to work a new route, 101 to Dover Castle. Further Guy Arabs were converted between 1968 and 1970, allowing the original fleet to be replaced as well as a further increase in services. For the 1969 summer timetable 101 was extended to Hythe, with a second bus working from Dover depot. The same season saw 69 extended to the new Hoverport at Pegwell Bay and right round the Thanet coast to Minnis Bay. Such was the

success of both these routes that they were further improved in 1970; 69 gained an half-hourly headway, absorbing service 56. Service 101 was also increased, to hourly, and extended alternately to St Mary's Bay and Lympne Airport (101a). 1971 was the zenith of East Kent's open-top services, with a second bus at Herne Bay for 45 Station to Reculver, although the St Mary's Bay leg of 101 was cut back to Dymchurch. For 1972 route 101/a was replaced by 121 a Folkestone circular, requiring just one bus; surplus vehicles were hired by Samuelsons to introduce open-top working on the London Transport Sightseeing Tour.

121 lasted only two summers, and no replacement was provided; similarly the second vehicle at Herne Bay lasted only one season, and ended entirely after the 1974 summer. This left only the Thanet service, now operated by the third generation of open-toppers, 1959 AEC Regents converted in 1972/3. Many journeys were lost in 1974, due to staff shortages, and this was reflected in the 1975 timetable when 69 was officially reduced to hourly. The service was converted to one-man-operation in 1981, with the introduction of the current fleet of two Leyland Atlanteans and a Bristol VRT. With the closure of the Hoverport the southern terminus became the Chilton Tavern, Ramsgate in 1983.

M & D Leyland-National KKL531P turns at Wormshill on the last day of M & D operation to this village.

An East Kent Bristol VRT/Willowbrook stands at Hastings on the long route to Dover introduced with the Shepway MAP scheme.
(M & D and East Kent Bus Club)

MAP SCHEMES

MAP — Market Analysis Project — was a system devised by Midland Red to produce a viable service network, with services over and above this level provided by local authority subsidies. It was based on a great mass of data which was processed by computer, an important part of which was an extensive passenger survey.

Many NBC operators subsequently made use of this system, including M & D and East Kent with the surveys taking place between 1978 and 1980. They were introduced on an area by area basis, with extensive publicity; many operators used 'local identity' fleetnames, but in this area the only example was the restoration of the Hastings and District fleetname. After a decade of fairly extensive service revisions, MAP produced even more dramatic changes; more rural routes were withdrawn and several new links were formed.

The Swale Area scheme was the first to be introduced on 3rd February 1980; M & D's Faversham Depot was closed, resulting in further operating changes with East Kent. The M & D operation to Herne Bay on 638 ceased, but East Kent worked a new market-day diversion to Canterbury, giving a direct service for the villages between Staplestreet and Yorkletts. Joint route 603 Canterbury-Faversham was extended to serve Oare and Bensted House Hospital covering the former town service 676, with alternate buses running through to Maidstone as 333. Major cuts were made to the rural services, with the loss of M & D 660 Faversham-Stalisfield Green and 661 Faversham-Chilham (ironically this former East Kent route was

in fact covered by an East Kent bus on its last day); both routes were replaced by Donsway of Dunkirk. From Sittingbourne cuts ended bus services to Tunstall (by the diversion of the Bredgar route via Borden), Oad Street and the M & D operation to Wormshill and Frinstead. Sittingbourne town services were recast, with several areas being linked on a continuous loop working — the 350, for example, running Kemsley-Chalkwell-town centre-Bell Road-Tunstall Gardens-town centre then returning to Kemsley — which were subsequently marketed as 'Sitti-circuit'. A new service was 340, a Friday link with Hempstead Valley for Sheerness and Sittingbourne. The same day saw the last conductors at Maidstone and Gillingham, as well as Sittingbourne.

This was followed by Gravesend and Borough Green areas on 13th April; key changes were the truncation of 322 Gravesend-Tunbridge Wells north of Borough Green, which became 222/3 and lost its Sunday and evening service, as did the Borough Green-Sevenoaks section of 9; new route 308 providing a two hourly headway between Gravesend and Maidstone via Borough Green, with a reduction of the traditional route via Strood (now 320) to one through journey on weekdays; 311 from Gravesend was extended beyond Meopham four times a day to Longfield — a partial restoration of a pre-1933 working; further south more buses were diverted via Vigo Village, a modern overspill development, but the nearby village of Harvel lost its five journeys a day, except for a school bus; the

Hastings and District RKO820M stands at Hawkhurst Bus Station prior to working the infrequent service to Hastings via Sandhurst; the bus is a lowheight Bristol VRT/ECW.

Gravesend terminus was moved from its traditional Overcliffe location to the Railway Station.

East Sussex County Council made considerable cuts to subsidies resulting in service reductions and the closure of Bexhill depot from 27th April, somewhat pre-empting MAP. These changes planned the end of M & D buses to Hooe, Little Common Road, Turkey Road, Cooden Drive, Ridgewood Gardens, Cantelupe Road, and under Sackville Arch, but at the last minute the council requested three services, 487-9, worked by one bus to cover some of these gaps, pending the start of the Bexhill Community Bus.

The next areas to be dealt with were Ashford and Shepway from 7th September 1980, resulting in the closure of Seabrook (Folkestone) and Cobbs Wood (Ashford) depots. The principal new facility was the jointly worked 550 providing a two-hourly service between Hastings and Dover via Rye, Lydd, New Romney and Folkestone, much improving the tenuous links across the marsh. The 551-9 group along with 550 gave a quarter of an hour service Dover to Hythe, splitting as 555 to Lydd via Lydd on Sea (alternate hours), 558 to Grebe Crescent (hourly), 559 to Saltwood (hourly with some journeys to Canterbury), and hourly short workings of 550 to St Mary's Bay.

On the debit side extensive rural cuts included 518 Hastingleigh's link with Ashford and Brook's only service, 519 Ashford-East Brabourne, with a Friday extension to Hythe, which in practice had only run fitfully towards the end, due to problems providing the mandatory Bristol LHS; 801/2, the remaining Harvey Hospital routes to Lydd/New Romney were withdrawn, releasing the Ford A for former M & D worked 404/24 to Smarden; new route 413 from Rye to the Hospital via Lydd and Dymchurch, gave a partial replacement. Romney Marsh communities to lose their services included West Hythe, Burmarsh and Snave.

Ashford town services were recast, with most routes becoming cross-town (only to be split again on 23rd November to counter late running) with Willesborough Lees, Henwood and Batchelors Factory becoming unserved; all routes became OMO, ending Regent operation on stage services at Ashford.

14th December 1980 saw the introduction of the East Sussex MAP, with some of the most vicious cuts ever. Notable features were the use for the first time of loose-leaf timetable folders in place of the traditional printed book, and the use of Hastings & District fleetnames on buses based at Hastings (Silverhill), Hawkhurst and Rye — the latter two were reduced to outstation status and the former East Kent premises at South Undercliffe, Rye, were closed.

Rural cuts included 248 Hawkhurst to Uckfield which was cut back at Heathfield with just three Monday to Friday journeys; 252/3 Tunbridge Wells to Hastings were withdrawn south of Heathfield, along with Sunday and evening trips — these routes had not so long ago enjoyed an hourly service. Other losses were: 257 Uckfield-Mayfield, 259 Burwash-Tunbridge Wells (Monday-Friday shopping service), 260 Wadhust-Lamberhurst-Tunbridge Wells, Saturday only 472 Hastings-Ponts Green and the Crowhurst leg of 471.

VJG192J, a Marshall bodied AEC Swift of East Kent on Deal town service 382 on the day before MAP and the closure of the depot which dated back to Deal & District days.

Because of delivery problems from usual manufacturers, both East Kent and M & D took Plaxton bodied Fords into stock in 1976 and 1977. They were withdrawn as part of the fleet reductions with MAP. The last ones worked from Edenbridge, including NFN324R, an East Kent example photographed at Tunbridge Wells in January 1982.

Former Dengate route 408 Hastings-Northiam-Rye was withdrawn south of Staplecross, leaving this section covered only by 254 Tunbridge Wells-Hastings which was itself greatly reduced south of Hawkhurst. One plus feature was the restoration of another old Dengate working between Rye and Hawkhurst as 405, albeit just one return service. Also withdrawn was 401, which provided peak service into Rye from Tenterden via Rolvenden.

Hastings town services were reduced, on some roads by half, and generally restructured, but the only sections to be totally uncovered were minor, like Pilot Road and part of St Helens Road. At Bexhill the routes introduced in April were withdrawn as they were now covered by independent services, and several more such operators commenced replacement routes in various parts of Sussex.

Sheppey MAP commenced on 4th January 1981 and included the closure of Sheerness depot, with the remaining twelve buses being parked overnight at the bus station. Cuts were especially heavy to the east end of the island, with 364 to Warden reduced from eight buses a day to a return school service. 341 to Maidstone was cut from four buses a day to a return service on Tuesdays.

The Medway scheme was introduced on 8th February resulting in a reduction of some nineteen buses, many from works and school journeys which were absorbed into standard routes; one unusual feature was the introduction of a special service network for Sundays, with routes numbered 120-8. No route mileage was lost, and indeed there was further expansion in the ever growing Walderslade to serve Beechen Wood and Fostington Wood estates. Many traditional links were severed and some new ones forged; for example 326 was further cut to run from Chatham to Sittingbourne only with some buses diverted via Upchurch and Lower Halstow (as 327). To compensate 135-8 Hempstead Valley to Chatham was extended to Gravesend, and marketed as Centrelink. Another fresh link was that from Grain and Hoo to Wayfield by the diversion of the 191 group away from its traditional Gillingham terminus.

Thanet MAP was introduced on 3rd May 1981 with a substantial reduction in frequency rather than areas served. Operation of AEC Regents ended and several routes were renumbered; also eliminated was the last letter suffix, 49a. Local objections were strong, including a proposed community bus service, which ultimately came to nothing.

A notable day was Saturday 25th July 1981, the last day of timetabled Regent operation and of Deal depot, prior to the introduction of MAP schemes for the rest of the East Kent area. Service losses included 399 Deal-Betteshanger-Westmarsh, 398 Sandwich-Aylesham (except for a Thursday shopping trip numbered 571), the 638 journeys to Canterbury only introduced with Swale MAP; several other services were drastically reduced like 622/3 Canterbury-Stodmarsh, and 667/8 to Charing. Deal area services were renumbered from the 3xx series to 5xx numbers, and the remaining Deal based buses were out-stationed from Dover, parking overnight in the bus station. One plus factor was restoration of the Hastingleigh-Brook-Ashford link by the extension of 620 from Canterbury on Tuesdays, Thursdays and Saturdays.

Maidstone MAP commenced on 9th August, and is dealt with in detail below; from the same date 601 Canterbury-Ashford was absorbed into 400 Ashford-Tenterden-Hastings, a move postponed from East Sussex MAP.

The final scheme, that for Tonbridge and Tunbridge Wells, was introduced on 21st February 1982 and again featured revised town service networks, with reduced frequency in some cases and further cuts in rural services. Total withdrawals included 251 serving Kilndown, 279 to North Farm Industrial Estate and 282 linking Southborough and High Brooms. At Edenbridge the remaining Village Bus services were withdrawn; E1, the town service, was absorbed into 236 to East Grinstead, and 234 to Tunbridge Wells via Cowden, which was cut to Holtye Common on most journeys to connect with 900 Gatwick-Gillingham. Vehicle withdrawals included the last of the Ford saloons; Tonbridge depot survived MAP, but was closed from 26th September, along with further service cuts, due to reduced subsidy payments from Kent CC.

Maidstone MAP included operation by East Kent's Ashford depot on the rural service via Pluckley; JJG8P, a Leyland Atlantean/ECW prepares to leave Maidstone High Street on such a working.

Maidstone area bus services

The Maidstone MAP was significant as it included for the first time a co-ordinated network of services jointly operated by Maidstone Borough Council and M & D. Although M & D have always carried local passengers the timetables were not integrated, resulting in some wasteful duplication and indeed the two operators even used different stops, causing the quaint local custom of waiting in between stops to see which bus came first! Co-ordination schemes had been discussed several times in the past, but had never come to fruition. The 1974 discussion did, however, result in the introduction of a new joint route (80) to Madginford via Shepway.

The new network commenced from Sunday 9th August 1981 and featured many radical changes. MBC buses began to serve the rural areas around the town, that had become part of the Borough following the 1974 local government reorganisation. Some M & D routes were diverted to serve the town's estates; their Maidstone depot was closed and vehicles were provided from adjoining garages, including East Kent at Ashford. To assist with this a number of routes were

linked across Maidstone: service 11 Maidstone to Mereworth became 111/2 and commenced from Gillingham; route 9 Maidstone to Sevenoaks was linked to route 10 Maidstone-Ashford-Folkestone; the new 10 included the through working of East Kent buses to Sevenoaks. Service 5 Hastings-Maidstone was restored to its old terminus at Gillingham, to allow the buses outstationed at Hawkhurst to be cleaned and refuelled. Further East Kent involvement was a share of 13 Maidstone-Pluckley with MBC, with the East Kent vehicle running to and from Ashford, and also the operation of many of the OAP free services. Vinters Park also saw some East Kent buses with the diversion of 333 Maidstone-Sittingbourne-Canterbury.

Ringlestone lost its local route in favour of diversions of alternate Gillingham buses; similarly the London Road/Headingley Road was covered by M & D's 71 group from the Larkfield/Snodland area, which was also diverted to Penenden Heath. These routes had previously served Bearsted which now had a new pattern of circular services (8, 18, 80, 88) running via Ashford Road, Landway, Bearsted Green, Madginford, Downswood, and Shepway with various permutations giving each area two or three buses an hour in each direction. These routes were worked by MBC and M & D, mainly from Tenterden with some Borough Green schedules. Some M & D routes were diverted to run odd trips via Park Wood and 82 Barming-Park Wood

Some town services were interworked with rural routes by Hawkhurst, resulting in Hastings & District fleetnames appearing. EKL456K, a Leyland Leopard with Marshall bodywork heads for Penenden Heath.

Bedford JJL/Marshall midibus HKX553V leaving Stoneborough Shopping Centre represents Maidstone Borough operation on the Village Link service.

also gained M & D journeys, including a Hawkhurst car running town centre to Park Wood all day Saturday. Former M & D local 89 to Coxheath was merged with MBC 81 Barming to Loose; new 89 included workings by MBC, Gillingham, Hawkhurst and Tenterden. The Barming leg of 82/9 was co-ordinated with M & D 6/7 to Tunbridge Wells to give a ten minute headway; on Sundays these M & D routes provided the entire service to Barming. An interesting new route was X76, which linked the housing at Barming with its rather remote station over a mile to the north; three journeys at commuter times were provided.

Tovil local route 87 gained M & D buses off-peak and at peak times it was covered by the rural routes from Horsmonden, Goudhurst and Yalding shared between Tunbridge Wells, Hawkhurst and MBC. New service 29 to Marden via Coxheath took MBC vehicles deep into the Weald, as did their workings on 59; this route was extended beyond Chart Sutton to Headcorn (the limit of MBC operation) and Tenterden, replacing some direct workings on route 12.

It was the rural routes to the south and east of Maidstone that were particularly badly hit, with many routes losing off-peak services. To compensate a network of Village Link buses was introduced to provide daily return shopping facilities plus a late evening service three days a week. Hawkhurst worked the day-time runs on the Horsmonden/Goudhurst/Yalding Village Links, and MBC (usually with a Bedford JJL) worked all the evening journeys and the daytime services on the Hollingbourne/Leeds/Grafty Green runs. The Dial-a-Ride service was further reduced, with the remaining journeys connecting with trunk routes at Tovil, Loose or Coxheath; similarly the eastern Village Link made connections for Maidstone at Bearsted or Hollingbourne Corner. These arrangements proved unpopular with passengers and so from 10th January 1982 these routes were extended to the town centre and at the same time new route 19 to Bearsted

Another rural route to gain Maidstone Borough workings was to Leeds; Bedford YQMS/Lex CKN332Y stands at Leeds Church.

Green via Ware Street partially restoring a facility lost with the withdrawal of M & D route 61 to Hollingbourne via Bearsted. The evening operation on Village Link was withdrawn in October 1982, after which the title was dropped from publicity.

Since MAP was introduced there have been several modifications to services, (for example the London Road has had two recasts; the first to counter late running problems and the second due to residents' complaints that too many buses were using the Headingley Road loop!) but the network remains basically unchanged. Since 1983 Maidstone has been reopened as a four vehicle outstation of Borough Green to reduce dead mileage.

MODERN INDEPENDENT OPERATORS

It was in South-East England that the territorial companies had most success in buying out the independent stage operators, with only three such firms of any size lasting to modern times within the area considered here. Indeed between 1974 and 1980 East Sussex was unique in being the only county without independent stage services.

In recent times the reverse has applied, as various operators have provided replacement facilities for services withdrawn by the major companies. These fall into two groups; existing firms diversifying from contract and private hire or new operators arising from groups concerned at the loss of various facilities.

THE SURVIVORS

The largest of the stage operators to continue until comparatively recently was John Dengate & Son. The first venture into passenger transport came in 1903, when John Dengate, then a baker at Battle, made good use of his bread-van on Sundays! By 1919 he was the owner of garages at Northiam and Beckley, with a small coach business. In 1922 a stage service began from Northiam to Hastings via Rye and Broad Oak using four small Napiers. Other routes from Beckley to Battle and Robertsbridge soon followed (although these ceased in 1935 and 1936 respectively) and they were later joined by the Rye-Hawkhurst service. After the war the Hastings route was diverted to run from Beckley direct via Broad Oak. The first double-decker arrived in 1949 and they remained a feature of the fleet, used mainly on school contracts, although they did sometimes appear on stage runs.

John Dengate died in 1957 and his son took full control of the business, after being a partner since 1929. A feature of the fleet in later days was the increasing age and poor condition of the vehicles, with many wrecks rotting at the depots as sources of spare parts. In February 1967, following a visit by the Traffic Commissioners, all but two buses were ordered off the road, with M & D providing temporary cover from 16th February on the stage services and Davie's Coaches of Rye working the school contracts. From May Davie also took over the stage operation still using the Dengate fleet-name, with two new Ford buses and some second-hand purchases.

From 12th February 1973 the services were recast as 1 Rye-Northiam-Hastings, 2 Rye-Northiam-Hawkhurst and 3 Hastings-Northiam-Hawkhurst; the section from Newenden-Hawkhurst ran only three days a week and was withdrawn entirely the following July.

From 5th May 1974 Davie sold the Dengate operations to M & D, with three Fords, four Leyland Leopards and a Bedford passing into the M & D fleet.

Another firm to fall foul of the Traffic Commissioners was Drew of Waltham. This business took on the services of the Chartham Bus Service in 1955; one bus was employed on a daily service from Canterbury to Chartham Hospital, with one of the coach fleet working a Wednesday and Saturday run to Chartham Hatch. The fleet was down to just two vehicles in May 1974, when both were ordered off the road for poor maintenance. Operations continued with hired vehicles until 9th December 1974 when the routes were taken over by East Kent; the Hospital service became 122/3, and Chartham Hatch workings 124.

Newman of Hythe was another long established operator, dating from the twenties, that operated a service from Hythe Sea Front to Ashford via Lympne, Aldington and Mersham. In 1963 a fleet of over ten buses and coaches were owned, but the firm decided, in view of falling profits, to concentrate on its furniture business. Operations ceased in May of that year, when the stage service (but no vehicles) passed to East Kent.

There were also a few minor bus services that were little threat to the major companies. Jessops of Frinsted was certainly running by 1938 and probably before 1930. In latter days they ran a single Bedford OB on a local school run, with a Friday only shopping trip to Sittingbourne. The firm ceased in 1973 and the service was not replaced.

A similar type of service still runs on Saturdays from Stansted to Gravesend, now worked by Horlock Coaches of Northfleet. As this firm only commenced in post-war years the route was presumably acquired from another business, possibly that of Pilgrim Coaches of Fairseat, which ran a service from that village to nearby Wrotham until 1955 when the firm ceased.

This Crossley/Willowbrook (DCT486) new in 1948 served Dengate of Northiam from 1959 to 1965; its poor condition can be seen in this view at the depot.
(M & D and East Kent Bus Club)

One of the buses supplied by Davie of Rye after taking over Dengate operations was SSD326, a Bedford SB with Yeates bodywork, a type rare in this area; it is seen at Rye in 1969.

Newman's 1945 Bedford OB/Duple, HKK593 waits at Ashford to work the service to Hythe. (M & D and East Kent Bus Club)

Drew's last stage vehicle was JAR622G, a Willowbrook bodied Bedford; it is taking a rest at Canterbury Bus Station on a quiet Sunday in 1971.

Latest Thames Weald stock includes PKR399W, a Dodge with Rootes bodywork; this view was taken on the new service to Maidstone in July 1984; it had just passed the factory where it was completed.

THE REPLACEMENT SERVICES –
THE WHEEL TURNS FULL CIRCLE

Thames Weald Travel Society began in 1961, as a non-profit making service organised by some West Kingsdown residents, using a hired minibus, to cover London Transport's withdrawn Sevenoaks-Gravesend route. This illegal operation soon attracted the attention of the authorities, but a road service licence was obtained, along with its own bus, with Dr H. Hefferman becoming the proprietor of the firm, which later became a limited company. In 1967 a new route from Sevenoaks to Romford via West Kingsdown and Dartford broke fresh ground and provided a partial replacement for the withdrawn London Transport facility through Dartford Tunnel. This route was extended in 1972 to Crawley via Edenbridge and Gatwick; this proved overambitious and was cut back to Sevenoaks again in 1976. In July 1984 some journeys were diverted on Tuesdays and Saturdays to serve Maidstone. Thames Weald have never operated vehicles larger than a 29-seater and a pair of Dodge midibuses are the current frontline stock; a former vehicle of note was MXX 323, an ex-LT Guy Special.

In the Liberal heydays of the sixties at Orpington there was much local pressure to improve bus services. As a result LT introduced 479 to Biggin Hill on Saturdays only from February 1963, but withdrew it in June; this provoked some local councillors to run a replacement service under the guise of the Orpington Rural Transport Association. This route was improved several times and by March 1967 it was running every thirty minutes with an hourly continuation to Tatfield or New Addington.

North Downs began a route to Croydon in April 1969 – another link LT refused to serve – again using minibuses, numbered service 853. It grew rapidly, reaching an half-hourly headway with limited Sunday service; it also provided a Sunday service to Ramsden Estate (854), which was served by LCBS 493 other days. A new estate at Forestdale, just off the main route, was linked with Croydon as 855. North Downs, who also had acquired some routes in the Guildford area, became over-stretched and abandoned 855 in July 1971. A new operator, Orpington & District, owned by Miss Normington who was also manager of ORTA, provided a replacement service; traffic increased needing double-deckers by 1975. North Downs cut 853 back to hourly, using 45-seaters, and withdrew Sunday workings in 1972. Meanwhile ORTA were in trouble, cutting back to Biggin Hill and folding totally in July 1975; the route was replaced by North Downs as 858. In early 1976 North Downs' licences were revoked for poor maintenance, and O & D took on the Orpington area routes, about the same time commencing a Biggin Hill to Croydon service, which was later suspended due to operating problems. The crash finally came in March 1981; Tillingbourne Bus, a long established operator in the Guildford area took on the Orpington-Forestdale-Croydon (ironically they had also acquired North Downs' routes at Guildford) and Crystals, an Orpington mini-coach firm, covered 858

Standing at Orpington Station awaiting the arrival of the train in August 1984 is Crystals' A691DMV (Leyland Cub/Reeve Burgess) on the service to Biggin Hill.

to Biggin Hill; subsequently Tillingbourne introduced a Forestdale-Bromley shopping service, but on 23rd September 1983 sold this part of the business to a new firm, Metrobus.

A further example of the instability of independent operations is shown by former East Kent 92 (Dover-West Hougham-Capel), which since withdrawal on 21st December 1976, has been worked by four different firms, Crosskeys, Folkestone, Johnson of Stanford, Hollis of Dover and the current operator Skelton of Dover, who took over from 3rd February 1984. The service is worked by a minibus with Tuesday and Friday shopping trips, plus school contract runs.

Post buses are now an important lifeline in many parts of rural Britain and there are a few routes operating in this area. They operate on marginal cost as the bus picks up and delivers mail en route, normally with two round trips a day. The first route in Kent was introduced on 23rd October 1972 from Canterbury serving the remote hamlets of Crundale, Sole Street and Thruxted, previously unserved by public transport.

The Sittingbourne to Frinsted, Milstead and Wormshill route began on 4th March 1974, initially supplementing M & D's facilities to these villages, which ceased with MAP. Other post buses run from Tunbridge Wells to Mayfield and Heathfield to Waldron.

Another novel minibus service was Denis Hire Cars' Dial-a-Ride service from Maidstone East to Coxheath, Loose and Boughton Quarries. This began in August 1972 with two Ford Transits providing a thirty minute headway, with the radio-fitted buses responding to calls to the control office from intending passengers. The service ran Monday to Saturday during shopping hours and evening, although there was a gap mid-afternoon when the vehicles worked school runs, helping to ensure the viability of the service. The service attracted much opposition from both the local bus and taxi operators, but the

The Crundale Post Bus waits to leave Canterbury Bus Station; the vehicle is CCD532L, a Commer with Rootes bodywork.

One of the two Dial-a-ride Ford Transits seen just after the operation had been purchased by Maidstone Borough, when it was still in its original orange livery.
(M & D and East Kent Bus Club)

licence was granted partially due to the experimental nature of the service; fares were set half-way between that charged by conventional bus and by taxi. From 5th July 1976 the service and both minibuses passed to Maidstone Borough Council; operation continued but suffered several cuts, losing late evening and Saturday services. In 1978 Forest Hill Estate was added to the service and the route was semi-fixed. With MAP, operation was cut to a few journeys only and from January 1982 the Dial-a-ride facility was dropped, by which time it had achieved the distinction of being the longest lasting of all such schemes across the country.

The West Kent cuts of 1978 resulted in a flurry of independent activity. From 1st April Camden Coaches of Sevenoaks replaced M & D 68 to Borough Green via Ivy Hatch and Plaxtol; former 96 to Fawke Common was also covered by double running. The service ran Mondays to Fridays only, with a second vehicle required to cover journeys at Wildernesse School. The route was soon cut back to Plaxtol, leaving Crouch unserved, but since then the operation has remained stable; from April 1984 some journeys were diverted to serve Shipbourne on Wednesdays and Fridays. Coaches were used to work the service, but in 1982 a Bristol LH bus was purchased to work the route. This is truly an example of the wheel turning full-circle as this route was originally worked by West Kent Motors.

Fage of West Kingsdown began a service to Swanley Station, also from 1st April 1978, as a partial replacement for the reduced LCBS service, but it lasted only until 22nd June.

From 28th April Meopham & Luddesdown Parish Council operated an experimental service between Meopham and Harvel on Fridays only, using a minibus hired from Reliance coaches at Gravesend. This route traversed some narrow roads via Luddesdown not served by the M & D route, which ran via Vigo. On 19th January 1979 a Community Bus Permit was issued, and the service was worked by Meopham Welfare Committee's HKK782D, a 10-seat Bedford converted from an ambulance, using volunteer drivers. At the same time the route was converted to a circular; with MAP Harvel lost most of its M & D service, and the community bus was introduced additionally on Tuesdays.

A second route was introduced on 25th February 1983 to Longfield, replacing M & D 310 and running on Fridays only — from this date the Harvel run was reduced to run Fridays again. From June 1983 the bus was also used for monthly shopping trips to Maidstone and Canterbury. The service was recast from 2nd March 1984 as a through Harvel-Meopham-Longfield-Gravesend route, still running Fridays only.

It was the MAP schemes that resulted in the greatest number of independent routes. As already mentioned Donsway entered the stage service business in February 1980, replacing M & D 660/1 using HKJ256N, a former Maidstone Borough Bedford. 661 (to Chilham, Saturdays only) ran only to July; from 26th July 1981 a Monday to Friday working was introduced on East Kent 637 between Dunkirk and Whitstable. From 5th September 1982 some 660 journeys were extended to Graveney to cover reduced services on East Kent 638; 661 was restored as far as Selling, but now running on Thursday, and new route 662 Faversham to Doddington provided a Wednesday and Saturday shopping facility, replacing the weekday operation on M & D 345. September 1983 saw further journeys introduced to Graveney and 661/2 amended to run on Fridays. Donsway are sufficiently proud of their stage service operation, which survives with minimal subsidy, to name their service buses Private Enterprise I, II etc.

By far the most important of the stage operators to appear in the independent sector has been Fuggle of Benenden. This long established firm, whose activities include running the village garage, have been operating coaches since the end of the war.

Much of the work was school contracts and the fleet reached a low of two vehicles in the mid-seventies, but expanded again following the arrival of Mr Wilmot as manager. Stage working began in a small way on 10th June 1980 with three rural shopping services, each with one return journey: Hartley-Kilndown-Hawkhurst (Thursday), Benenden-Iden Green-Rolvenden Layne-Tenterden (Fridays), Biddenden-Benenden-Cranbrook (Tuesdays). The network was expanded considerably from 14th December 1980, with route 1 Benenden-Rolvenden-Rye replacing M & D peak facilities on 401; this route also provided a thrice weekly shopping service for Bodiam; route 2 provided a Monday only Sedlescombe-Hawkhurst link in addition to M & D 254; the original Friday service became route 3, with 4 providing a new facility to Maidstone Market on Tuesdays from Sandhurst via Benenden and Smarden; 5 gave a Wednesday Bodiam to Tenterden service, with 6 & 7 providing market day (Thursday) service to Rye from Appledore and Bodiam respectively. All these routes were covered by one bus and a Bedford saloon, JKN61N, was acquired from Maidstone for these routes. All this proved slightly ambitious and, after some minor alterations in January,

Camden Coaches' Bristol LH/ECW (GLJ492N) with a standing load of school children at Seal in April 1983.

HKJ256N Donsway's ex Maidstone Borough Bedford YRQ/Willowbrook waits in Faversham to work to Stalisfield Green, while the coach behind will run to Graveney.

The most basic form of public transport; Bedford HKK782D, a former ambulance, works the Meopham Community Bus in April 1983.

the network was reduced to just routes 1, 3, 4 and 7 (which now started from Benenden) from April 1981.

The next route developments came with Tunbridge Wells MAP on 22nd February 1982, when a second bus was required to work route 15 Benenden to Brenchley via Goudhurst and Paddock Wood at school times, and new 2 Benenden-Kilndown-Tunbridge Wells off-peak, both replacing former M & D workings. Among the new facilities was route 9, a Wednesday only run from Hawkhurst to Canterbury via Biddenden and Pluckley.

The third stage vehicle was required from 7th September 1982 for 8 Benenden-Horsmonden-Tonbridge for West Kent College students, with three weeks later rural routes being further revised to include a Friday service to Leigh Green on route 3; and also on routes 2 & 10, including through workings to Tunbridge Wells on the former.

During the 1983 Summer Holidays advantage was made of the lack of school commitments to offer some longer stage routes: 5 Benenden to London via Horsmonden on Mondays, 11 Matfield-Eastbourne on Tuesdays, 12 Matfield to Folkestone on Fridays; also 7 was extended to Camber and 9 to Howletts Zoo, thereby giving the Wealden villages a different day-out option for the whole week. Similar facilities were offered for 1984.

Fuggle's expansion has been closely guided by Kent County Council and on the vehicle front closely associated with Maidstone Borough, who have sold them four machines, one of which was unfortunately lost in a depot fire in 1982.

Fuggles also operate buses from the Maidstone Borough fleet, but this Duple bodied Ford (NCY269R) came from South Wales, and was photographed at the Beneden depot.

From January 1982 Westerham Coaches have operated a school-day service 485 from Sevenoaks to Chartwell via Westerham and Edenbridge, replacing LCBS facilities.

On Sheppey, Piper provided a Sheerness-Warden Bay facility from 13th April 1981 until 25th January 1984, when the fleet was put off the road by the Traffic Commissioners and operation reverted to M & D from the 28th.

Johnson of Stanford replaced two East Kent routes from 7th September 1980, the 518 to Ashford via Brabourne (Tuesdays and Fridays) and 813 Mersham-Lympne-Folkestone (Thursdays); the former lasted until 21st July 1981 when East Kent operation was restored over part of the route and the latter still runs, but since 6th January 1983 has been worked by Poynter of Wye.

The latest stage operator to appear in Kent is New Enterprise of Tonbridge, which took over part of 222 Tonbridge-Borough Green and local routes to Barden Park and Brook Street from M & D with effect from 1st August 1983.

In Sussex the first independent service appeared on 1st September 1980 when Rambler Coaches of Hastings restored the Bexhill-Hooe service. It was, however, on the local routes that much interest was centred; first to appear was the Bexhill Community Bus, which entered service on 15th September 1980, using volunteer drivers, and gave a Monday to Saturday service to four areas which had lost their M & D service; 1 to Cowdray Park Road, 2 to Pebsham Lane, 3 to Glovers Lane and 4 to Ridgewood Gardens via Sutton Place.

Manxtree, trading as Bexhill Town Bus Service, commenced operation on 8th December 1980 and was one of the first operators to take advantage of the Transport Act, 1980 to gain licences for routes that competed with both M & D and the Community Bus. This was a new firm formed by six M & D men who worked at the former depot, and because of this their identity remained secret till the last moment. Rother District Council provided the capital to buy a fleet of former Plymouth Leyland Nationals. Nine routes requiring three buses were worked to Sutton Place, Ellerslie Lane and Mount Idol at Sidley, Little Common via Cooden or Sackville Road and an Old Town/Ridgewood Gardens circular. From 7th November 1981 Mr Harmer, owner of Renown Coaches, took a 75% holding in Manxtree, and subsequently the fleet has been replaced by more reliable Leyland Panthers from Eastbourne Borough. On the service front the situation has remained remarkably static, although the Community Bus has withdrawn from Glovers Lane, sending route 3 to Cooden Beach instead (from 9th March 1981) and also left Ridgewood Gardens to Manxtree (9th February 1982).

Hastings was first reached by Monk's Coaches of Staplecross with a Friday service from Bodiam via the hypermarket. Coleman, a St Leonards taxi firm was next, with a Hastings-Battle minibus service, which restored bus operation to Crowhurst and was supported by County Council grants. Operation commenced in March 1981 with three trips a day; from September the bus also worked a town service to St Helens Cemetery via Elphinstone Road, with five trips providing a part replacement of the hourly pre-MAP service.

Ford, a Netherfield shop-keeper, entered the bus business on 22nd January 1981 with a weekdays Heathfield-Battle service again worked by a minibus. This was extended to Hastings (St Helens) via Crowhurst and the hypermarket from 2nd August 1982, thus duplicating Coleman mileage — ironically Ford was paid a subsidy to run to St Helens competing with Coleman's unaided route!

OGS800V, the Bexhill Community Bus Ford Transit/Reeve Burgess on service at Bexhill Station in February 1984.

The same day saw former Eastbourne Leyland Panther/East Lancs at work for Manxtree.

Pook Hill Taxis of Burwash Weald began a weekdays Burwash-Heathfield service on 1st December 1980 (replacing M & D 248), a Thursday shopping journey to Tunbridge Wells (replacing 259) and to Eastbourne alternate Saturdays, again worked by an ageing minibus. Within a year the main route had been extended to Hurst Green, but reduced to three days a week. A Wednesday run to Hastings from May 1982 lasted only a few months and other routes declined until operations ceased in October 1983.

Ford, whose own route was now reduced to Saturdays and school-days south of Battle, covered Heathfield-Hurst Green on Tuesdays only; but from 30th April 1984 Rodemark of Herstmonceux began a grant-aided Mondays to Fridays service.

Both Ford and Coleman ceased to operate in June 1984, with Rodemark providing replacement facilities, save for the Monday to Friday off peak service between St Helens and Crowhurst which passed back to NBC operation by Hastings and District. From 2nd September 1984 Rodemark also replaced the Hailsham Postbus service.

Olsen JFD285V (Ford/Duple) waits at Bressenden Place, Victoria during the first week of commuter coach operation in October 1980.

A Pilchers of Chatham Bedford/Duple VVD435S covering an Olsen working heads along the Embankment in January 1982.

THE TRANSPORT ACT, 1980

The 1980 Transport Act was part of the Thatcher Government policy to promote free market forces and private enterprise and made the first major change in the law relating to road service licensing since the 1930 Act.

This Act resulted in the deregulation of all operations, tours or express coaches, where passengers were wholly conveyed over thirty miles; the only requirement was to notify the Traffic Commissioners twenty-one days in advance of starting the service. For stage service operations obtaining new licences was made easier and providing it was in the public interest, protection of the existing operator ceased. In practice few operators have tried to compete in this field, where subsidies rather than profits are the rule; there have been some exceptions to this, notably at Whitehaven and Cardiff and, within this area, at Hastings and Bexhill (as already covered).

Predictably it was the express coach services that have increased dramatically, especially commuter runs to London, although not all routes or operators have prospered. There had been growing pressure for commuter coaches for some years, as new housing was located away from stations and improved motorway links with the capital offered faster journey times; such proposals were usually scotched by the railway on the grounds of abstraction. Since the Act the number of such services to be developed has been staggering, with some subsequently being converted to stage carriage (as much to obtain fuel tax rebate as to carry short distance passengers) and licences have also been granted to firms to run in from areas less than thirty miles out. With a few exceptions all the commuter routes from Kent run over Tower or London Bridges into the City then run to Victoria via the Embankment.

THE OLSEN SAGA

One of the firms to run from the first possible day, 6th October 1980, was Olsen Coaches of Strood. They had a large modern fleet and had recently lost part of their contract work to the industrial sites on the Isle of Grain. Some market research was done with the aid of a local free paper and with their spare vehicles they were able to offer a number of routes with relatively compact pick-up zones.

Initial routes were from Hempstead and Wigmore; Miers Court and Parkwood; Grain; Earl Estate and Knights Place and also Ashford. Fares on the Medway services were initially £1.25 single £11.25 weekly season ticket; however they were quickly reduced (to £1 single) to equal M & D's rates.

Growth in the Medway area was rapid and, although the Ashford run soon ceased in favour of Swinards, by mid-November eleven coaches were running. This included two coaches from Maidstone and one from Sittingbourne; more and more coaches were gradually introduced until a peak was reached in the summer of 1981. By this stage Olsen were getting into trouble; vehicles were spending all day in Vauxhall coach park and all night parked near drivers' houses — and thus few were being properly maintained. Revenue was also depressed by competition and this meant that the lease payments on the fleet could not be covered and so some older coaches were acquired. All this resulted in breakdowns, complaints from commuters and the attention of the Traffic Commissioners. To cover vehicle shortages coaches were hired from many firms, especially Pilchers of Chatham and Grey-Green, London, N6; both soon experienced problems obtaining money from Olsen and so retained the fares taken on their coaches. From 28th September Saxby of Strood took over the route from Sittingbourne via Rainham with two almost new coaches.

One of the coaches drafted in by M & D to cover the rail strike and the Olsen collapse was East Kent Leopard/Duple PVB800S, seen at Bressenden Place in February 1982.

The scale of the operation is shown by the November 1981 timetable, which showed twenty-nine vehicles serving Grain (coach 1), Frindsbury (2), Lordswood (3, 16, 21), Chatham (16), Rainham (5, 12, 14), Cuxton (4), Hempstead (7, 15), Lower Gillingham (8), Maidstone, Allington (10), Bearsted (11), Cliffe Woods (13, 20), Wayfield (18), Vigo feeders (22, 24), Meopham (23, 25), New Ash Green (27, 29), Hoo (28), Upper Gillingham (30), Higham (31), Gravesend, Valley Drive (32), Upper Higham (33).

Peter O'Neill's Kingsferry Coaches took advantage of Olsen's problems to start their own commuter services from the Rainham/Parkwood area on 12th October 1981. Valedene Coaches took over the two Maidstone coaches (10/11) in December and Grey-Green took over the Vigo/Meopham workings from 4th January 1982, and a week later the Hoo and Cliffe Woods runs.

Olsen finally folded on 15th January 1982 with debts of over £400,000, part of which was owed to commuters for season-tickets. Just five days after this Olsen was already due to appear before the Traffic Commissioners to defend the continuance of its operators licence; instead Mr Allen, the Olsen director, applied to start a new firm with fifteen coaches, which was refused. There was much confusion for the next few weeks (especially as the railways were troubled by one day strikes at this time) as various operators fished for Olsen's traffic.

Grey-Green took over most of the remaining services west of the Medway, using ex-Olsen drivers but with the coaches being maintained in the daytime at their Stamford Hill garage. Valedene tried for a short while to work the Grain route, and the New Ash Green commuters formed themselves into a club which hired three vehicles from Turners of Harrow, driven by their regular Olsen men.

On the other side of the river M & D and Kingsferry workings were increased and Horlock's of Northfleet and Garden of England Coaches, Gillingham both entered the market for the first time, although the latter withdrew in favour of Kingsferry after two months. Pilcher's Coaches also continued to run five vehicles on the workings they were covering for Olsen; it is of interest to note that Pilcher's have been in business since 1859, and for many years ran the horse bus service from Luton to Strood before concentrating on coach work. Saxby also got into trouble and ceased running during the tail-end of 1982, again in favour of the expanding Kingsferry services. Recently operations have been more stable with Kingsferry and Grey-Green both employing over a dozen coaches each day and smaller operations by Horlock and The Londoners complete the current independent sector workings from the Medway area. Pilcher's pulled out of this operation from June 1984 after some problems with the Traffic Commissioners.

OTHER INDEPENDENT COMMUTER SERVICES

Many other firms have also entered this highly competitive market with some finding a viable traffic flow, but others have foundered, especially some of the early entrants to the field.

Smith's Coaches of Sittingbourne was running by early November 1980, and continues to work from Sheerness and Teynham via Sittingbourne using five coaches.

Swinards of Ashford began running from 3rd November, with the last pick-up at Lenham and the coach running through to Gloucester Road coach park. Initially it was advertised with four coaches with on-board refreshment, but it has never reached that level (except during the 1982 rail strikes) and now runs with just one coach.

The Bexhill based Renown Coaches started a service thence to London on 3rd January 1981 and also from Hastings the next month, but both soon faded away.

Regent of Whitstable did a trial service in 1980, but did not attract enough custom; they tried again with the rail troubles of early 1982, this time starting from Herne Bay with a feeder from Sturry via Canterbury; this enjoyed a modest success, but it ceased in September 1983.

Nu-Venture Coaches of Maidstone also tried a service in October 1980. They had a second attempt from 2nd November 1981 starting from Coxheath and running via Loose and the Tonbridge Road. This was later joined by a Willington Street starter and both still run. Towards the end of 1981 a number of new routes were started; the success of these was guaranteed by the industrial trouble on the railways in early 1982. The first of this group was the West Kingsdown Coaches facility serving East and West Malling, Wrotham and its home village with two coaches, although this was subsequently reduced to one vehicle and was withdrawn after 1st June 1984.

2nd November 1980 was a popular day for new services with Valedene of Sutton Valence beginning a Headcorn-Maidstone-Larkfield run and no less than three operators starting routes from the Gravesend area — Reliance of Gravesend, Olsen and also Green Line 720. In December Valedene took over the Maidstone runs from Olsen, but these ceased from 16th June 1983 following M & D's improved services, leaving only a modified version of the original route, this too ceased after 10th February 1984. Reliance's operations have continued to expand, especially after the Olsen collapse, and today, some fourteen coaches run from Higham, Milton and River View Estate, picking up through the town en route.

A third independent to enter the battle for the Maidstone area traffic was D H Coaches of Lewisham, who instigated routes from Bearsted Green via Vinters Park and Park Wood via Larkfield on 7th December 1981. A Barming-Wateringbury-Paddock Wood-East Peckham run failed to attract enough travellers, as did the Saturday journey from Park Wood. D H's routes were attacked by the increased M & D service in March 1983, and they pulled out after a few months' competition.

A Kingsferry Volvo/Plaxton sets down at Temple in November 1983.

Coaches gather and almost block Bressenden Place, Victoria ready for the evening rush home during the rail strikes of February 1982; nearest the camera a Garden of England Coaches vehicle, then a Grey-Green coach on the Grain route and on the far side a D H Coaches vehicle on the Maidstone service; all are Bedfords.

The rail strikes in January and February and again in June and July 1983 gave rise to many extra coaches and routes; many were only temporary but some survived, including New Enterprise Coaches of Tonbridge running from Crowborough via Tunbridge Wells (with a feeder from Frant and Pembury added in February 1983), and Interland Coaches of Orpington serving the Green Street Green and Farnborough areas.

Two operators serving the settlements between Dartford and Gravesend are Clearway Coaches of Eltham (Greenhithe and North-fleet) and Centaur of Sidcup (Southfleet and Bean).

At the time of writing over fifty commuter coaches from the local independent operators are working into London — the Transport Act has certainly had a major effect in this area.

Carrying a special headboard for the Herne Bay commuter service is East Kent's OKE137P, a former M & D Leyland Leopard with Duple coachwork. (M & D and East Kent Bus Club)

Heading over London Bridge to Gravesend is Green Line PFN791M, an AEC Reliance that had earlier passed from East Kent to National Travel South East when carrying Hoverlloyd colours.

NATIONAL BUS COMPANY OPERATIONS – EAST KENT

East Kent have developed few routes arising out of the 1980 Act; two commuter coach routes were introduced on 2nd November 1980, the 996 from Folkestone (Cheriton) via Hythe and Ashford, and 997 Herne Bay (Beltinge) via Whitstable and Faversham; 996 soon ceased, but the 997 found enough support to continue and indeed a second coach was later added; from 5th April 1983 this was revised so that 997 ran fast from Whitstable, with the relief coach becoming 998 from Herne, picking up through to Faversham.

East Kent also worked part of a through Dover-London-Birmingham express service during the 1982 summer season, although it was not repeated in 1983. Generally the London to East Kent coach routes have seen increased custom and improved frequencies, but one interesting new route introduced on 20th June 1982 was 025, joint with Green Line and Southdown; it ran every three hours between Dover and Portsmouth running via Canterbury, Chatham, Gatwick and Brighton. In January 1983 it was extended to Bournemouth with additional operation by Shamrock & Rambler; it was further revised in September 1983 when the Kent end was diverted to Ramsgate. By using the motorway, journey times are much improved over the old South Coast Express (now 026) timings, and this route has accordingly declined – the winter 1983 timetable has just three trips a week from Dover to Brighton.

A second link with Brighton is limited stop 718, from Canterbury via Hawkhurst, again joint with Southdown, which started on 5th May 1982.

GREEN LINE

The Green Line operations have also expanded rapidly as a result of the new legislation, but much of this is beyond the scope of this book. In Kent the first post-Act change to the Green Line network was ironically a negative one, for on 21st April 1981 the majority of journeys on 706 Tunbridge Wells were cut back to Bromley. A new link started from Gravesend to Crawley via Bromley, Croydon and Gatwick as service 755 on 13th June 1981, although the Kent end was withdrawn after less than a year.

One route to be successful is 720, the Gravesend commuter coach, which commenced on 2nd November 1980, restoring the link with the capital – this time as an express service. Since then it has gone from strength to strength and now includes an hourly regular off-peak service and extensive duplication on the commuter timings.

Not all of the commuter routes have been successful; 721 from Dartford lasted only from 5th April to 14th May 1982. The same number was also used for a journey which ran from New Ash Green on 21st January 1982, after the Olsen crash, but only attracted six passengers. From 16th May 1982 a number of odd-day tourist orientated routes were introduced for the summer season; one running into Kent was 728 serving Penshurst Place and Hever Castle from Victoria. With effect from 31st July 1982 a fast London to Tunbridge Wells via Tonbridge service (756) was introduced joint with M & D, but this only lasted until the end of the year.

In Victoria Coach Station in FKM718L, one of three Leyland Atlanteans M & D converted to coach standards to work Invictaway services. This 1982 view shows the now discontinued black with red sash livery.

INVICTAWAY

The growth of M & D's Invictaway network has been the most spectacular of all post-Act services in this area. This was the marketing name adopted by M & D for a new group of limited stop services between Medway and London introduced on 6th October 1980. Main routes were 991 from Parkwood and Gillingham via Strood and 992 from Gillingham via Luton, Lordswood and Walderslade; each ran daily every two hours, and were supplemented by commuter routes 990 from Grain via Gravesend and 993 serving Wigmore and Rainham. The bargain fare of a £1 single was charged and the service was co-ordinated with National Express 005 (Sheerness-Sittingbourne-Gillingham-London); minor alterations made from 16th November included the first up 005 becoming 995, and 990 being diverted by Strood rather than Gravesend.

Further improvements were made from 17th May 1981, when the last down journey was diverted via theatre land and an early up Sunday coach with a lunchtime return was diverted via the commuter route serving Aldgate for Petticoat Lane market.

On the commuter coach side 990 was withdrawn, as Olsen had cornered the market, but 994 was introduced from Murston and Sittingbourne. In September 1981 the remaining 005 timings were made 995s.

During 1981 two other routes were added to the Invictaway marketing name, these were 919 Tenterden-Maidstone-Swanley-London (an amalgam of the old 035 express and Green Line 719 Wrotham-London dating from 1st April 1978) and 900 Gillingham-Gatwick Airport via Maidstone, West Malling and Tunbridge Wells running every two hours from 6th July 1980. The 900 has since been dropped from this group of services.

The network was greatly expanded from 2nd February 1982 following Olsen's demise, with 991/2 both becoming hourly and a number of new commuter timings being introduced. The 994 started from Eastcourt, leaving the Sittingbourne area commuter traffic to Smith's Coaches; 988 served Luton via Davis Estate and 989 Otterham Park via Rainham. Timetabled peak coaches now reached ten, but with the rail strikes in 1982 duplication was frequent. Another peak variant to appear during the year was 987 from Borstal via Delce, starting from 4th July.

On the vehicle front three coaches were painted into a special black promotional livery during 1981 and later that year it was decided to convert three of the 1972 Leyland Atlantean double-deckers to coach standard, again painted black. During the strikes many double-deck bus extras were run, and the demands for additonal coaches for Invictaway work has resulted in such vehicles being hired from East Kent, West Riding, Ribble and Southdown and the purchase of second-hand Leopards from Fox of Hayes.

Displaying the new green and white stripey livery is GKK159V, a Willowbrook bodied Leopard on the Maidstone service.

The latest Invictaway vehicles are five impressive Leyland Olympians with ECW coachwork, such as GKE443Y seen at Gillingham; Green Line also have some of this type on their Gravesend service.

The first development of 1983 was the introduction of 956, a commuter service from Tunbridge Wells (Rusthall), as a partial replacement for 756. More substantial was the launch of a much increased Invictaway service from the Maidstone area on 27th March 1983. An hourly service fast Lewisham to Lunsford Park splitting at Maidstone for Parkwood (980) or Bearsted (981) on alternate hours was provided. Sundays and summer weekdays certain 981 journeys were extended to Leeds Castle.

The 919 was withdrawn south of Maidstone and replaced by 980 Tenterden via Headcorn and 978/982 via Cranbrook; there were several variations to this pattern, mainly at commuter times, especially as M & D forced out pre-existing operators. Various alterations were consolidated from 16th October, when 980 was diverted to run via Cranbrook, leaving the Headcorn road to Valedene coaches. Currently